From

The Women's Press Ltd
34 Great Sutton Street, London EC1V 0DX

Best wishes
from
[signature]
Dec 1998

Isha McKenzie-Mavinga is a professional counsellor, specialising in developing training courses to include the experience of black people, especially black women.

Thelma (Tod) Perkins is trained as a nurse and as a teacher, particularly interested in language development of the under-fives. Both live in London.

ISHA McKENZIE-MAVINGA
THELMA PERKINS

In Search of Mr McKenzie

Two Sisters' Quest for an Unknown Father

The Women's Press

First published by The Women's Press Ltd 1991
A member of the Namara Group
34 Great Sutton Street
London EC1V 0DX

British Library Cataloguing in Publication Data
McKenzie-Mavinga, Isha
    In search of Mr McKenzie: two sisters' quest for an
    unknown father.
    1. Great Britain. Social life, 1901–– Biographies
    I. Title   II. Perkins, Thelma
    941.082092

    ISBN 0-7043-4249-9

Typeset by MC Typeset Ltd, Gillingham, Kent
Printed and bound in Great Britain by BPCC Hazell Books,
Aylesbury, Bucks, Member of BPCC Ltd

Dedicated to our sister Lynda, our family,
children and our children's children

Contents

Acknowledgments

Thanks and acknowledgment to:
Our editor Akwe Amosu. All our family and friends who
have supported, encouraged, and been very patient with
us. Alex Pascall, the LeMaitre family, Dr Charles Ward,
Adewole John, the Busby family, Mrs Toussaint, the late
Mrs Rodriguez, the late C L R James, Dr William Besson,
the British Museum Library, the British Museum
Newspaper Library, Ernest Marke, SuAndi and Tom, Kath
Locke, members of the West Indian Sports and Social Club
and the West Indian Ex-Servicemen's Club in Moss Side,
Berry Edwards, Ferdi Blanc and family, Sam and family,
Val Jones, Mr and Mrs Trotman, Joan Riley, Lord Wilson
of Rievaulx, Roy Hattersley MP, Lord Pitt of Hampstead,
Mrs Roy Chase, Mr and Mrs Onslow, Kath Lyndon,
Pauline and John Grey, Patsy Potter, Ebun, Jenny
Harrison, Jenny McKenzie, 'Auntie' Kathleen Richardson,
the late Bella Cooper, the Calabash Club in Lewisham, the
Rector of St David's Anglican Church in Plymouth,
Tobago, Peter Fryer, Roy Sawh, Cecil Gutzmore, Len
Garrison, Mr Burns and Dr Malcolm Joseph-Mitchell.
Many thanks also to Bernice Johnson Reagon for allowing
us to use her song *Mae Frances*.
We were financially assisted in our research by Lewisham
Leisure Services and the Arts Council.

Chronology

125 years of Herstory

1876	Birth of Mary, our grandmother
1892	Arrival of Mary in England
1893	Marriage of Mary to Aaron Hartz in Liverpool
6 December 1898	Birth of Ernest Nicholas McKenzie in Trinidad
21 August 1912	Birth of Elise Hartz, our mother, in Birmingham
c. 1916	Marriage of Ernest to Catherine Eugenia in Trinidad
1914–1918	First World War
21 April 1925	Birth of Lynda, Ernest's eldest daughter
1930	Ernest arrives in England
28 May 1938	Marriage of Ernest to Elsie Hart in Birmingham
1939–1945	Second World War
24 October 1939	Birth of Andrew Arthur Cipriani to Ernest and Elsie McKenzie
13 November 1941	Birth of Teddy Albert to Ernest and Elsie McKenzie
8 October 1942	Birth of Thelma Mary to Ernest and Elsie McKenzie
February 1943	Andrew, Teddy and Thelma are placed in the Chislehurst home
October 1943	Ernest returns to Trinidad

21 November 1945	Fifth Pan African Conference in Manchester
10 November 1948	Birth of Jane Susan to Ernest and Elsie McKenzie
25 March 1949	Death of Ernest
May 1949	Jane is placed in the Brockley home
c. 1950	Elsie remarries
1954	Thelma returns to Birmingham
December 1955	Jane goes home to Birmingham for her first visit
January 1956	Family home in Sparkbrook collapses and the family is rehoused in Ladywood
1957	Thelma starts her first job
1959	Thelma leaves home to live in London
10 November 1962	Thelma marries
1965	Jane leaves the children's home and starts work
September 1967	Death of Elsie
1968	Jane marries
1980	Jane gets divorced
1979 and 1980	Thelma and Jane begin to study for degrees
October 1982	Thelma and Jane visit Dr Ward
June 1983	First letter from Lynda
August 1983	Lynda and her husband visit London
February 1984	First journey to Trinidad
1983 and 1984	Tod and Isha graduate
1985	Second journey to Trinidad
1989	Third journey to Trinidad
1990	We finish the book

Dear Sir or Madam,

I visited London last week with the object of calling on you for the purpose of making arrangements for handing over three children of Jewish connection to you, if there be room in your homes. The following are the facts. My wife is a Jewess, and I am a Negro. The two races are classified as inferior by Hitler, and my race is so classified by all other peoples in the world, including the English. Although I have produced a good home wherein I hoped to bring up my children in accordance with the Christian practice, I find that the home is on the verge of breaking through pressure put on my wife by her family members who are bitterly prejudiced against my complexion. My wife declares that she finds it wholly impossible to care for the children, and so I must find somewhere to put them . . .

E.N.McKenzie

1
Elsie's Story

Grandmother Mary was born in 1876 in Kovno, then in Russia (it is now called Kaunas and is in Lithuania). Her Jewish parents died when she was a baby and a farming family who were friends of theirs brought her up.

She came to Britain when she was 16 with her two brothers, who shortly afterwards emigrated to America and disappeared from her life. A year later, in about 1892, she met and married our grandfather, Aaron Hartz.

He was also an immigrant who had sought refuge in this country from the pogroms. He was a master tailor and worked hard to support his growing family. The family was to live in Paris, in London and in York before finally settling in Hurst Street, in Birmingham's Jewish quarter. Mary and Aaron had 14 children, one of whom was our mother. She was born in 1912 and they named her Elise; but when her birth certificate was filled out the registrar misspelled her name and she grew up as Elsie.

Only two years after her birth the First World War began. Our grandfather was classed as an alien and interned in a camp on the Isle of Man, even though three of his sons were fighting for Britain at the time. Mary would have been interned too but was allowed to remain at home because of her young children. Conditions in the internment camp were terrible. Aaron was so disillusioned by the treatment he and other internees suffered that soon after his release he left for New York to join one of his sisters, inexplicably leaving his wife and children behind.

Mary was in her fourteenth pregnancy when Aaron deserted her. Her last two children were twins: one died and the other, Zena, survived but was physically disabled and died in the early 1960s. One of Mary's sons died during the war, and the health of the other two was affected by the gas used in trench warfare, and when Mary sought help for them through the British Legion, she was told to go to the Jewish Board of Deputies. Mary stayed in the Hurst Street area of Birmingham where there were many other Jewish families and although she did not keep up a strict observance of Jewish customs, Elsie remembered that she would still light the Sabbath candles each Friday evening.

Life was hard for the family between the wars. Mary was left struggling to bring up the younger children, the older ones having left to join Aaron in America. Our mother grew up poor. She was only about six years old when her father left, and to help Mary she would scrub doorsteps for a farthing and go to the Bullring market late on a Saturday afternoon to pick up the fruit and vegetables left behind by the stallholders. At Christmas time they received food parcels distributed by the Cadbury family.

Elsie was extremely short-sighted and attended a school for partially sighted children for a while, only joining her brothers and sisters at the local school later. She left school at 14 and trained as a French polisher in the furniture trade; when she was about 18, however, she went to work with one of her sisters, Bella, in the kitchens of the Wesleyan General Insurance Company. She was probably 24 when she met the father of her first child; he was a Londoner who disappeared from her life very quickly, leaving her with a baby daughter, Sheila.

In those days – the late 1920s and early 1930s – Birmingham boasted several large dance halls and Elsie loved to go dancing, often with her sister Bella. They would finish work and hurry home to change, discussing clothes and partners, and Elsie would arrange for someone, usually her mother, to look after her young daughter. The sisters worked long hours in the company kitchen and going dancing shook off the drudgery.

It was during one of the dances that Elsie loved that she met Ernest in 1937. She and Bella had not seen many coloured people; they knew of a few Indian doctors setting up practices in the city and they had seen one or two Africans who were studying at the college. Ernest must have swept Elsie off her feet: perhaps he wooed her with tales of Trinidad. Elsie had known only poverty until now and probably hoped that at last life was going to improve.

They were married on 28 May 1938 and Elsie's daughter Sheila took Ernest's surname. In October of the following year, as the rumours of war became reality, she gave birth to their first son, Andrew Arthur Cipriani. After a brief stay in Hockley, the family moved to Handsworth where, for a short period, Bella moved in to keep Elsie company while Ernest travelled. He was often away and Elsie was unhappy: she was expecting another baby and found Ernest's long absences and the lack of money, combined with the stress imposed by the war, difficult to cope with. They moved again, this time to Sparkbrook, to rooms above and behind a tailor's shop. Ernest, meanwhile, rented a room in Handsworth to use as an office.

In 1941 another son, Teddy Albert, was born. Within two months Elsie was pregnant again. During her pregnancy she was often on her own, and with three young children. Eventually, after Ernest had been absent for several months, she placed the children in the municipal children's home at Erdington. But when she went to visit them she was appalled at the state they were in: all three were dirty, with runny noses and heads full of lice, and her daughter Sheila had rheumatic fever and was very ill. She took the children home.

As the birth of the next child became imminent so the intensity of the German bombing raids on the city increased. One night, as an exhausted Elsie slept, she was awakened by the sound of the sirens. She struggled with the three children to the air raid shelter, only to find it locked. As her panic mounted, a warden came and informed her that what she had heard was the 'all clear siren. She trundled back with the children stumbling along behind, and after that experience she found it easier to shelter under the kitchen table.

Ernest was away when his third child, Thelma, was born: Elsie went into labour while she was alone with the children. She strapped 11-month-old Teddy into his pram and went next door to ask her neighbour to contact the midwife. On her return she found the toddler hanging almost unconscious over the side of the pram: in her haste to summon help she had only hooked the harness to one side of the pram.

Ernest often went away on business for short periods and would return to find his wife distressed and barely able to manage. When Thelma was four months old it was decided that the children should be cared for by someone else. However, Elsie was adamant that they were not to be returned to the municipal home in Birmingham. Ernest wanted to send them to Trinidad and began making arrangements for the journey; but Elsie protested and refused to let the children go so far away, and she reminded Ernest of a home in Chislehurst in Kent where some of her sister's children had stayed for a while.

The children's home in Chislehurst was for children of Jewish origin, but children were taken in on the understanding that they would be given a Christian, not a Jewish, upbringing. The society that ran the place, The Barbican Mission to the Jews, was dedicated to saving Jews from being Jewish.

Children arrived there under various circumstances. Some were Jewish refugees rescued from a war-torn Europe, and flown to Britain on a plane chartered by the

Barbican Mission to the Jews.

"NAOMI" HOME.

Application for Admission.

Name of Parents

Father _Ernest Nicholas McKenzie (Mavunga)_

Mother _Elsie McKenzie_

Address of Parents _66, Stratford Rd, B'ham, 11._

When Married _28th May 1938_

Where Married _Birmingham Registry_

Name of Child _Thelma Mary_

Boy or Girl _Girl_

When Born _~~18th November~~ 8th October 1942_

Where Born _66 Stratford Road, Birmingham, 11_

Are there any other Children? _Yes_

If so, how many? _3_

And what are their ages? _5 1/2 yrs, 2 1/4 yrs, 1 1/4 yrs_

Father's Trade _Teacher & Journalist (At present unemployed)_

Father's Nationality _British_

For what reasons do you wish to place the child in the Home _mother's_
inability to care her through indifferent health

Are you willing that the child be brought up in the Christian Faith until he,
or she is 16 years old? _yes_

What amount per week are you willing to contribute towards the cost of your
child's maintenance? _One pound per month (£1)_

director. There were abandoned children, one or two whose mothers had given birth to them in prison or in other desperate circumstances, others who had been left in the care of a relative who no longer wanted them. And there were children like us whose parents just couldn't cope.

Parents had to sign an agreement committing their children to the home until they were 16 years old. The contract stated that the children would be brought up in the Church of England, instructed in the Christian faith. Many refugee parents, desperate to get their children to safety, signed. Later, some of those children were taken away to be cared for by relatives or by people who were practising Jews.

Ernest wrote to the director and, as soon as Thelma was five months old, arrangements were made for the departure of the children: Sheila, Andrew, Teddy and Thelma. Elsie, who had been parted from the children before, could not bear to make the journey, and so Ernest travelled south with them and signed the agreements which committed them to the care of the home.

For the next six years Elsie remained at home and, although she did accompany Ernest on some of his journeys around the country, she still had to spend long periods on her own. From 1942 until 1948 Ernest frequently travelled to Trinidad, although he never revealed the reason for his visits.

Once the war had ended the children were able to spend short holidays at home in Birmingham, and Ernest often visited them in the children's home or would meet them in London to take them to the zoo.

Early in 1948 Elsie discovered that she was pregnant again, and in November – Ernest was away again (in a letter after Jane's birth he mentions having just returned from 'a tour of the north') – she gave birth to another daughter, Jane.

History was now to repeat itself: grandmother Mary had

been left fatherless as a very young child; Elsie had been deserted by her father at the age of six and, when Thelma was six years old and Jane only four months old, Ernest died, leaving Elsie in severe financial straits.

She decided to send baby Jane to join the other children in the home. She probably hoped that all her children would be together; however, by the time Jane went the structure of the home had altered. During the war all the children and staff had been evacuated to Devon and when they returned from there a smaller house in south-east London provided a home for some of the children while others remained in the much larger house in Chislehurt. Thelma stayed in Chislehurst and Jane was placed in the London home and for almost 18 years, other than for the occasional visit, they were separated.

The Barbican Mission to the Jews.

DIRECTOR:
THE REV. I. E. DAVIDSON, M.A.

Hon. Treasurer:
E. W. DAWSON, ESQ.

TELEPHONE:
IMPERIAL 80.

"SEVEN TREES,"

LUBBOCK ROAD,

CHISLEHURST, KENT

Dear

We are making every possible effort to reach the
thousands of Jews in our land, with the message of the
Gospel. Workers - men and women - are being appointed as
soon as their services become available to us; centres are
being opened up in the larger cities, and wherever Jews
congregate.

In seven centres where our missionaries are regularly
active, they find the ground very hard, but they are all
full of hope that with persistent prayerful effort the ground
will soften, and the good seed sown will bring forth fruit
to the glory of Christ our Saviour. Already a number of
conversions are on record. The past year has witnessed a
definite advance. Another three centres have been
established; thousands of Gospels and New Testaments and
tracts were distributed. Visiting house to house is an
important feature of the work. Open air services,
evangelistic meetings, prayer meetings and Bible classes,
Women's Meetings, Sunday Services and Sunday Schools,
children's meetings during the week are some of the items of
activity. A great number of Jews, as a result, are
considering the claims of the Lord Jesus. The Continent
demands our attention, and as the way opens up, we must be
ready to take advantage. The need is great and the
opportunities must not be let slip unheeded.

Your past fellowship with us in the ministry of the
Gospel among the Jews was of inestimable benefit to many
souls. Your prayers and gifts are held in remembrance
before God Who will not forget your service of faith and
labour of love.

I need hardly say that in our estimates to carry the
work forward, we rely on your continued co-operation, and
we know you will not fail us.

Yours in His Service,

2
Thelma's Story

Mount Zion, the house in Chislehurst which was the children's home, was staffed entirely by single white women, whom the children called 'aunties' and, apart from the director of the home, we rarely had contact with men.

The aunties were quite young, although to the children they seemed old. They were all committed Christians, dedicated to saving our souls as well as being responsible for our physical welfare. They came from all over the country to work at the home, having been recruited through the mission's work in other cities. They had no formal training; the only qualification appeared to be a desire to 'serve the Lord' and a liking for children. Working in the home and looking after us was a kind of pre-vocational training before going on to missionary training college.

Their days were long, as they rose before us and only retired to their own rooms once we were all in bed. They usually had a few hours off in the afternoon on a rota system and took it in turns to attend the local church for the service on Sunday evenings. They accompanied us when we went to summer camp and were all expected to work through the Christmas holidays.

Our cook was German. We were all fond of her but Home Office restrictions, while allowing her to cook for us, prevented her from looking after us like the other aunties. She came to work in the home soon after the end of the war, as did another European auntie, an extremely tall, very quiet woman whose job it was to do the mending. The cook worked for the mission until she retired, as did the auntie whom I was closest to, and with whom I still maintain contact. She began working for the mission in the 1930s as a 19-year-old country girl straight from a position in service and when the war ended she became housekeeper and cook for the director and his wife who lived in 'Seven Trees', the large house situated further down the road. She was the auntie who cooked for everyone when we went to camp and whose tent we all wanted to share. She looked after and nursed both her employers until they died and, unlike some of the other aunties, she never left to marry and raise a family of her own.

Wide white steps led up to the glass doors of the house and into the hall. On the left was the reception room, on the right was the girls' sitting room, half the size of the boys' common room which was next door. The walls of both rooms were lined with books and with banks of wooden lockers for the children's personal belongings: these lockers were the only private space we had.

The house felt like a stately home. The doors had brass knobs, brass finger panels and a brass door bell. In each room beside the fireplace was a bell that in years past had been used to summon the servants, and now was disconnected. Down in the basement were many more rooms – a wash room, a boot hole where all the shoes were kept, a cloakroom, a sewing room and a utility room where the ironing was done. There was a pantry with one whole wall lined with a huge dresser holding all the crockery, and cutlery boxes filled with knives, forks and spoons. The kitchen was enormous with a low ceiling and small windows. The dining room was also in the basement, a long room that ran the length of one side of the house; in it there were deal tables covered with tablecloths, each seating eight children.

Upstairs was the prayer room, filled with rows and rows

of polished chairs and kneeling cushions, where morning and evening prayers were held every day.

Outside there was a large garden, ideal for young children. We could hide and pretend not to hear when called to come indoors. There were blackberries, wild raspberries, hazelnuts and sweet chestnuts for us to gather, wild flowers to pick and vinegar leaves to search out and chew. There were foxes that came out at night, their screams piercing the dark and the dreams of the children sleeping on the two upper floors.

An enclosed bridge ran from the first floor of the main house to the staff annexe, behind which was a small chapel; on the other side of the house was a large wooden building, used as a gymnasium. Here the children played table tennis, swung on a trapeze and vaulted over the large wooden horse.

The house and the garden were wonderful for young children; but there were no parents.

Every Sunday without fail I filed down the road with the other children to the parish church. We walked in twos, each holding a partner's hand, neat and tidy in white socks and clean shoes, the girls wearing hats. My favourite was a Fairisle beret which I wore only on a Sunday.

My strongest memories of the home are centred on the seventh day and being 'saved', in order to go to heaven. On the long Sunday afternoons we sat quietly and carefully coloured in Christian texts with crayons: 'Though your sins be scarlet/They shall be as white as snow.' In Sunday school and during morning and evening prayers, I sang with gusto: 'Oh wash me in the blood of the lamb, and I shall be whiter than snow.' I was a little black girl with short, black curly hair and I wondered if I really would turn white when washed in blood. I sang loudly, I enjoyed the rousing choruses, Jesus loved me, oh yes He did. Or so the aunties told me. I confessed to loving him and I wanted to go to heaven when I died. What was death? Where was heaven? We pointed to the sky when we sang and knew only that

God saw everything we did, good and bad.

Did he see me the day that my father brought my brothers and I to the home in Chislehurst and left us there? Was he watching when all the children and staff were evacuated to Devon for the duration of the war to be safe from the bombing? (It was there that I took my first faltering steps while the staff and children were assembled to listen to the King's speech on Christmas day and, while stumbling across the room, wet myself and the cord of the radio, thus cutting off King George VI in mid sentence.)

Another early memory is of praying each night that my mother would give me Humpty Dumpty as a birthday present and receiving instead the largest ball she could afford (years later she told me that she had scoured every likely shop in Birmingham, but to no avail); and another still is of eagerly awaiting the parcels of liquorice allsorts, jelly babies and pear drops that she had sent my brothers and me.

One day I was taken to the optician to get a pair of glasses, and I remember afterwards on the way home trying to jump the ditches I could see in front of me.

'Ditches, what ditches?' asked the auntie accompanying me, before light dawned and she explained that it was the lower rim of my spectacles that I could see and that I would get used to them. And I did.

I read anything and everything, including the Bible; I even learned 100 Christian texts just to receive a postcard of the Light of the World, 'knocking at the door of my heart'.

I lived in a larger-than-life family until I was nearly 12 years old and I know I got more attention than the other children. I often went to 'Seven Trees', the director's house, on Saturday afternoons, to visit their housekeeper, the auntie who had mothered me as the youngest child in the home when I had been evacuated with the other children; I played in the kitchen, I followed her into the garden, I cooked real food and stayed for tea. She used to take me out for cream teas and make me dresses which were the envy of the other children; in the spring we picnicked in Knole Park and picked primroses in Paddock Wood; in the summer I went on holiday with her and visited her family and friends in Bristol and Berkshire.

We slept in the large, unheated, uncarpeted bedrooms. In the middle of a cold winter night the bathrooms and toilets seemed miles away. Our lives were regimented: rising in the morning when the bell rang, stripping and airing the bed, being ready for breakfast when the bell rang, making the bed before I left for school. We walked to and from school in the terribly cold winters. My chilblains burned and itched and someone would rub Iodex ointment on them for me, but sometimes they were so bad I couldn't put my swollen feet into my school shoes. On such occasions I could stay indoors and read books, curled up in a huge old armchair beside one of the fires, at which, on other days, the big boys roasted chestnuts stuck on to knitting needles. I envied the big boys: they rode bicycles all day, especially in the summertime, and played mouth organs.

In the summer we all went to camp, and when that was over some of the children went home to spend time with their own families; others, like my brothers, Sheila and I, sometimes went home and other times stayed in the home. During those long hot summers I played outside all day, in the garden or on the waste ground next door, building dens in the wild rhubarb and playing hide and seek.

Considering that we rarely heard a radio, we were pretty au fait with the songs of the postwar period. The house and garden would echo to the sound of 'On Top of Old Smoky', 'You are My Sunshine', 'Down in the Valley' and 'White Cliffs of Dover'.

On Saturday afternoons, when it was hair-washing time, I went with another child to buy a quart of vinegar, used for rinsing our hair. We used the change to buy an Oxo cube to nibble on the way back and used to drink some of the vinegar, carefully topping the bottle up with water back at the home before handing it over.

Later in the day I sat in the boot hole, taking my turn to polish shoes supervised by an older child. After that one of my favourite big boys would tell me stories about Freddie the Flea to help pass the time while we peeled the potatoes. We all took it in turns to do the chores: peeling potatoes, buttering bread, washing up, cleaning shoes in the boot hole; we got through mountains of potatoes, slice upon slice of bread, hundreds of plates, cups and saucers, knives, forks and spoons, rows of shoes, sandals and boots in all sizes and colours. In the kitchen I would seize the chance to lick the knife to taste real butter, before it was mixed with the margarine, and we would line up for doses of malt and cod liver oil each day like children all over England after the war, before sitting up to tea together where mountains of bread and butter melted like snow, washed down with tea, already milked and sugared, poured out from huge enamel teapots.

After the war my father began to come and visit me. Once when it was time to say goodbye, instead of leaving me behind, he asked permission to take me back to Birmingham for a while. He bought me two oranges outside Paddington station. Oranges were scarce then and I had never seen them before. I carried them carefully, one in each hand, and no one could take them away.

When we arrived in Birmingham my mother was delightfully surprised to see me and I was spoilt and pampered by everyone. Her brother, my uncle took me out, to the pictures, to the dog track, and to the shops. I was showered with sweets and money and so much attention. At the end of my stay my mum travelled back to Chislehurst with me, spending some time with my brothers and older sister before returning to Birmingham.

There were other times when my brothers and I were taken to Paddington station and put on the Birmingham train in the care of the guard. Often as we waited for the arrival of the train, a familiar figure strode into the waiting room to greet us. Ras Prince Monolulu was a well-known tipster and a friend of our father. He wore traditional African dress and a headdress of bright feathers in a turban, and was a familiar figure at race courses throughout England, where the punters paid him to tell them the name of a winning horse. I read his autobiography entitled *I Gotta Horse* a few years later. He began it by saying that he had been born in Ethiopia, 'A few hundred miles up the road from Addis Ababa.' In his youth he had walked across the country to the coast, and boarded a ship, and become a sailor. When he left the sea he made his home in London, where he became a celebrity tipster. He was most famous at the Derby at Epsom Downs, where he would appear in his costume shouting 'I gotta horse!' He was a generous man, and whenever we met him he would give us some money and wish us well.

I was always petrified when the train arrived. I hated the noise of the steam engines, the smell was terrible and they were so terrifyingly big. Once on the train, however, I settled down and looked forward to seeing my parents again.

There were pleasures to be had in the home. From October – when I stirred the Christmas pudding and wished – onwards, there was an air of anticipation. I remember waking on Christmas morning, sensing the specialness, listening for the arrival of the adults bearing the large tin bath heavily laden with long black, grey or brown stockings, each filled to the brim with goodies.

Unknown to us, every item in each of our stockings had been selected personally for its recipient. All through the previous year as gifts and donations were sent in, the wife of the director (having consulted her lists) would mark off an item against a child's name and drop it in the stocking which would be hanging labelled on a hook on a coat rack.

This way she made sure that we usually got what we had wished for and that gifts were never duplicated.

We sat on our beds to empty our stockings of the small toys and the food, a bar of chocolate, a tangerine and some liquorice. After that we went to church, and then ate a traditional Christmas dinner before Father Christmas arrived. Another present. Then traditional games and a treasure hunt, and then tea! Later we performed a short play and sang carols beneath a huge tree lit with real candles. Then, joy oh joy, I received another present – usually the one I had wished for earlier in October.

Sometimes – another pleasure – I walked to Chislehurst station on a Saturday afternoon and caught the train to St John's station on my own, to visit my little sister in the other branch of the home in south-east London. I was only eight years old but I would proudly push Janey out in her pram, waiting patiently as old ladies patted her head, ooh-ing and aah-ing over her. After tea I would make the journey back to Chislehurst.

After the Christmas holidays it was time to go back to school, filing across the common, all wanting to hold the auntie's hand, because, like most children, we had a bogey man to fear. Smoky Joe, the local tramp who rode a bike, could be heard long before he was seen. His bicycle had no tyres, no brakes and no lights or horn. He rattled along the roads that ran through the Chislehurst commons, the creaking bike heralding his approach. In the winter when the wind whistled through the trees and the frost lay white on the ground, he fastened a brazier of burning coals to the front of the bicycle to keep him warm. When I heard Smoky Joe coming, I hid behind the trees trembling, afraid that he would see me and steal me away.

Another person that I feared was Mrs Fairweather. Her house stood on its own on the hill and all the children were afraid of her. She was an old white woman with grey hair and she looked just like the witches in our books; it was rumoured that she locked children up in her toilet.

The staff maintained discipline by forbidding us to go out or by docking our pocket money. For the boys the ultimate punishment was the cane: they would be sent down to the director's house with a message and he would administer the strokes on their hand. I was once punished by not being allowed to go to my own birthday party. I was recovering from mumps at the time. All the other children were at school and I would not stay in bed. A workman in the house reported me to a member of the staff and I was warned what my punishment would be. I took no heed, however, and the party went ahead without me; I remember my brothers bringing me a piece of my own chocolate cake.

One evening after prayers instead of going straight upstairs for my bath I was allowed to stay up late and play. About an hour afterwards I was called, with my brothers and older sister, into the reception room. The director's wife sat upright on the same chair that she sat on when she dispensed sweets to us. She called us to her and put her arms around me. The others sat down close to her. She told us that she had some sad news for us. Our mother had written to her, our father had been ill in hospital. Our father had died. There was a silence. My older sister began to cry. So did my brothers. I did not understand what being dead was, so I sat still and watched. The director's wife prayed for us and our mother and said that we would see our father again one day in heaven.

We left the room and I was sent to get ready for bed. As I lay in the darkness with the other children whispering across to each other, I was still pondering about death. Then someone called out to me.

'Is it true that your daddy is dead?'

'Oh yes,' I replied. And I began to cry.

One of the aunties came and put me into bed with my sister in the older girls' bedroom.

26th

29 MAR 1949

R.66 Stratford Road
B. Ham 11

Dear Mrs Davidson,

Just a few lines to say I have some very sad news for you. My Husband passed away yesterday March 25th please break the news gently to my dear Children as I am too heart broken to write to Sheilah. I would not be able to tell her he was asking for her when he was dying. This was all very sudden, only ill three days with Phemonia. I will write more later give my love to my Children. Tell them I have written to you.

Yours faithfully
Mrs McKenzie

Burial Frid. April 1st 2 o'clock.
Perry Barr
B Ham

Mrs McKenzie   29 March
B66 Stratford Road
Birmingham, 11

My Dear Mrs McKenzie,

Your letter certainly gave me a great shock. I had to read it
twice to really take it in. I wish I could tell you how deeply
grieved for you I feel. You must indeed have felt most
stunned by the quickness and suddenness of such
bereavement.

I shall undertake the very sad task of telling the children all
together this evening. It is not an easy thing to do and you
know that I will seek for words as loving and gentle as I
can. Thank you for writing to me so promptly.

We have been remembering you in prayer already this
morning since your letter came, and shall continue to do
so. For those whose trust is truly in Christ there is no death,
and I would like just to pass on His own words. 'I am the
Resurrection and the Life: he that believeth in Me, though
he were dead, yet shall he live: and whosoever liveth and
believeth in Me shall never die.'

With very real sympathy from Mr Davidson and myself,

Yours sincerely,

   I was six and a half years old when my father died in
1949. I had last seen him the previous Christmas when I
had gone home for two weeks, when I had also seen my
baby sister for the first time and helped to choose a name
for her (soon after he died she too was placed in a
children's home). My father had taken us out during that
holiday and had given us a lot of his time. I was never
going to see him again.

A few years after our father died our mother remarried. Jimmy was a Barbadian who had grown up in Trinidad. Although he was a tailor by profession, before the war he had travelled to Panama and America, returning to Trinidad to work in the oilfields, driving trucks for the American company that administered the oil business. He had arrived in Birmingham soon after the war ended and had been introduced to Ernest.

The house on Stratford Road had plenty of room. There were four rooms upstairs which were rented out to men from the Caribbean. They had no difficulty in letting the rooms as overt discrimination by landlords was rife at that time: it was common to see notices in the windows of lodging houses with the legend:

No children
No Irish
No coloureds

Ernest used to meet the boat train when it arrived in London from Southampton and would greet new arrivals there; if they needed accommodation he would take them to our house in Birmingham.

Jimmy had been one of those new arrivals and, when Ernest died, he was still lodging in our house, and was probably the only person who offered our mother comfort and friendship. He asked her to marry him and, perhaps because she was alone, she accepted, for better or for worse.

In 1951 our mother gave birth to another daughter, Jimmy's child. Jimmy had, by this time, realised that he could not make a living as a tailor, and was working in a factory some distance out of the city. He continued to make suits for his friends, however, and for a while this supplemented his income.

Shortly after the birth of Elsie's seventh child, another girl, the last lodger moved out of the house. The only income now was Jimmy's, and so although our mother now had a partner who lived at home, she was still having difficulty making ends meet. The accommodation in the house was reorganised to meet the demands of the new family and she wrote to the director of the children's home asking for me to be allowed to come home.

I was 12 and very happy to pack my box, collect all my books and travel to Birmingham to be with her. My memories of holidays spent at home were good: being spoilt by her and my father, going out with my uncle, getting rides on his motorbike, getting sweets, hugs and, most importantly, attention.

Our home was behind and above a shopfront which during the war and until the mid 1950s was a tailor's shop. It was in a row of other shops, with accommodation behind and above. To get to the back of No. 66 we had to walk through a wooden gate and down an alley for about 50 yards, then turn sharp left and left again, past a large shed where I often played, past an eight-by-four-foot patch of earth – 'the garden' – past the coal shed and the outside toilet, to arrive finally at the kitchen door. I suppose we were fortunate to have so much room because many people were still living in cramped back-to-back terraced houses with shared outside toilets and no bathrooms. We also did not have a bathroom, nor did we have an inside toilet or hot water; but there were four bedrooms upstairs in that three-storey building, with two rooms and a kitchen downstairs.

I was used to hot and cold water in the taps and an inside toilet. I could have a bath whenever I wanted in the large bathroom at the children's home. At home, though, the toilet was outside. In the winter the pipes froze and when I bathed in a tin tub in front of the fire or in the kitchen the water had to be heated on the stove in kettles and saucepans. Later, when we moved to Ladywood, I used to rise early on a Sunday morning and go to the public baths.

There were no trees in our backyard or flowers. There was barely enough room for me to skip. The garden in

Chislehurst was large enough to build a complete housing estate on.

In Chislehurst there were walls lined with books, here I had to join the public library and return home to bury my head in my chosen book while the radio played and the little ones chattered on the floor.

There are letters which show that my mum wanted and needed me at home to help her, and this I did willingly. I washed up, helped with the babies, did the housework and ran errands, one of which gave rise to an interesting incident.

One day, while waiting to be served by our local green-grocer, Mr Capsey, a woman tried to jump the queue.

'Excuse me, but my friend is before you,' said Mr Capsey.

'Why doesn't she go back to where she came from?' retorted the irate woman.

'Well . . . she could, but I don't think it will be far enough for you!' he said, and proceeded to serve me.

On another occasion, I had accompanied my mum on a visit to my grandmother. As I sat opposite her on the crowded bus on which there were several people standing, a woman remarked, 'I wouldn't sit on a seat a coloured person had sat on for all the tea in China.' I held on tight to my little sister who was on my lap and looked at my mum; she had the baby on her lap and another sister sitting beside her.

'Don't worry love,' my mum told the woman, 'she isn't going to get up for you or anyone else.'

My mum later told me that she recalled an incident while travelling with my father on a Midland red tram during the war, when he stood up to offer his seat to a woman, who refused it. Mum said she had told him that if he did that again she would leave him: she couldn't bear to see him humiliated in public.

I was enrolled in the local girls' secondary modern, Highgate School on Upper Highgate Street. I was the only black girl, I was as middle class as the teachers who taught us and my accent was definitely not Birmingham. I was at a distinct disadvantage when school drama productions were being cast: I was always the witch or the black king in the nativity play.

One year the play decided upon was *The Bluebird*. My lines were the longest and I learned them with enthusiasm. However, there was some consternation about my 'refined' Kent accent and gradually my speaking parts were reduced from several pages to a few lines. I should have learned from experience: the previous Christmas I had spent hours in the cloakroom with one of my few friends, Margaret, trying to make 'baby' sound like 'babby' in order to present my gift to the Christ child in the nativity play. My attitude towards learning defied any of the stereotypes about black pupils that later emerged, as I was a voracious reader – which was uncommon enough in most pupils at that school – and I was therefore given access to my teacher's personal books.

My mother never talked to me about periods and was probably relieved when I announced to her one morning that they had started. She gave me a piece of elastic, two safety pins and some strips of torn-up sheeting. Each month these soiled rags would be soaked in bleach and then boiled, ready for re-use: I never used commercially produced sanitary protection until I was able to afford my own.

Life at home was so different from living at Chislehurst. Apart from running errands, helping with the little ones and going to school, I listened to the radio, bought my own sweets and books and often went to the local picture house, the Alhambra, where I and my cousin Peter paid 1s. 6d. (7½p) each. On Sundays I would take the younger children to the park, pushing them in the pram.

One Christmas Teddy and Jane came home for the

holidays. It was the first visit that Jane had made to our house since she had been taken to the children's home. I was proud to show her Birmingham and take her to the pictures to see *The Wizard of Oz*. However, that was the only visit she ever made to the house in Stratford Road.

One lunchtime I went shopping. It was a chill January day in 1955. I saw the dust rising down the road as I stood waiting in a queue at a shop. I assumed it was fog or smoke and skipped blithely back with the vegetables for the stew. Nothing had prepared me for the devastation that greeted me. Our home had collapsed like a pack of cards. My mum, Jane, Teddy and the two little ones had all been in the back of the building and were safe, very shocked, but unhurt. The man who owned the building, Mr Garrett, had instructed his men to demolish a load-bearing wall, in order to enlarge the shop premises below our home. The whole of the front of the building was gone. We never spent another night in that house.

One of the things that I had loved to do was to go up into the attic and look through the things that had belonged to my father, all stored away and waiting for me to be grown up enough to have them as my own. His writing, his books, his history. Now all of my father's life had disappeared with the rest of our home in the rubble.

We spent that night sleeping on mattresses on the office floor of the factory opposite the site where once our home had stood. The next day Birmingham Corporation rehoused us in a terraced house in Ladywood. It had a tiny backyard with an outside toilet; we had no bathroom or hot water and, although these conditions were similar to those at our previous home, this house was much smaller and I missed the attic where I could retreat and browse through a book.

I began school almost immediately at Camden Street School for girls. It was here, for the first time that I could remember, that I was hit for doing nothing wrong. I had not had time to make friends with anyone yet and we were in the art room awaiting our teacher, Mrs Gilmore. All the girls were already paired off and were busy continuing their assignments from the previous lesson and, as I had always been told that if I couldn't find anything to do I should read, I was sitting at my desk reading when the teacher entered and asked me what I was doing. As I replied her hand whipped out and landed with a resounding clap on my cheek. I know that I cried and that some of the girls comforted me. My mother never did anything about it, although today she would probably have seen the teacher in court.

Once again I was the only black girl in the school. The only one who read whenever she got the chance and the only one who was not apparently from a working-class background. Once again I made only a few friends, one of whom – Sheelah – I remain in contact with to this day, and with whom I probably shared the confidences that I would have shared with a sister. She had two brothers and a mother who always made me welcome.

I used to enjoy visiting our relations with my mum. We used to take two buses and make the journey across Birmingham and out to Selly Oak where Grandma Mary lived or Bourneville were Auntie Bella lived. I would help out with the younger children while tea was prepared. Tea at grandma's or at Auntie Bella's was a special occasion, and we always took a contribution towards it. There would be tinned salmon or a Jewish treat of pickled herrings, cold meat, salad, fruit, jelly and plenty of homemade cakes. The bread was spread with the best butter and I could have as much jam as I wanted on it. When we left my uncles would give us 2s. 6d. – one shilling for me and the remainder to be divided between the little ones.

During those years that I lived at home I continued to wear secondhand clothes. My mum's sister in New York regularly sent parcels of clothes to be shared between my cousin and myself, and we were fashionable in a way that no one else was. Girls at school envied me my clothes, not knowing that even my bras were secondhand. I don't think I realised how difficult things were for my mum and stepfather and how welcome those parcels were. I did have a new coat and a pair of shoes, purchased with the aid of a Provident cheque, a form of credit. The 'Provident' man would call each week for a payment which would include interest.

I continued to be my mother's right hand. I rarely answered back and always did as I was asked. From the time that the house collapsed both my mother's and my stepfather's health began to deteriorate. My mother was often ill in bed with various unspecified ailments, and therefore I ran errands, I minded the children, I cleaned the house and went to school. In church I still sang loudly, 'Yes Jesus loves me'.

I left school and began work as the first black clerical employee of the Birmingham Co-operative Society; I was a punch-key operator. After six months I was called into the managing director's office and asked if I was happy and got on well with my colleagues. I was informed that they had never employed a Jamaican before! My father was from Trinidad but I did not bother to enlighten him.

My friends were the girls who were on the Power Samas machines closest to me: Beryl, Pauline and Hilary. We would sit tapping away, at the same time singing the latest hits by the Everly Brothers, Paul Anka and Cliff Richard, priding ourselves on our ability to sing in harmony. It was with Hilary that I went to my first live concerts: the Platters and Ella Fitzgerald. Beryl and Pauline were the first people to call me Tod – they said I reminded them of someone they had known called Toddy McKenzie.

All the girls were curious about my hair and, at first, would pat it whenever they got the opportunity; later, when they realised how much it annoyed me, they stopped.

They wanted to know how I managed it, whether it hurt when it was combed and whether I got nits. For the first time in my life my hair was growing. My friends were amazed when I arrived proudly at work one morning with my hair straight. My first boyfriend had taken me to a friend of his mother who had subjected me to the Vaseline and hot comb treatment, and advised me what oils I should use on my hair and what cream to put on my skin. I continued to visit her and have my hair done there until I left home.

I struck up a friendship with a black maintenance man who worked in the Co-op buildings, and who was many years older than me. For months I and my younger sister visited him and his family in Handsworth and I had my first taste of real Caribbean cooking. Afterwards I would discuss the meals with my stepfather and he would sometimes recall other foods particular to Trinidad cooking.

I met my first boyfriend when he spoke to me at the bus stop one evening after I had been to a friend's house. I was not aware that our skin colour was the attraction between us. After that he even came to our house to meet my mother before we went on our first date. Two things used to mar those outings: before I went out I always had to do the washing up, and I always had to be home by 10.30 pm. I don't know how many films I watched without seeing the ending – if I arrived one minute after the allotted time mum was out there on the front doorstep calling my name.

At the age of 17½ I went to London and began to train as a nurse. I had begun to find life at home intolerable: no matter what or how much I did for my mum it seemed I couldn't please her. A combination of the menopause and her vague illnesses made her irritable, and she found fault with small things. I would do my best to please her, even taking time off from work to care for her and the children.

Events came to a head when she complained that I hadn't cleaned the grill on the cooker one Sunday afternoon. It was the one and only time I ever answered her back. She slapped me and I threw the dishcloth at her. I did not speak to her for two weeks while I negotiated a return to London with the wife of the director of the children's home.

My mother could not believe that I was leaving. She never apologised, but she did offer to come to the station with me – if I would help her do the washing at the launderette first.

In September, just before my eighteenth birthday, I moved into the nurses' home of the Queen Elizabeth Hospital for Sick Children on Hackney Road, which was later to become a branch of Great Ormond Street Hospital. There I began to train for a career.

My contact with my younger sister Jane increased, as I was able to spend all my off-duty time at the children's home where there was a room kept for visiting ex-residents, and I visited from east London at every possible opportunity.

I would occasionally go to a local club in the basement of a large house a few roads away from the children's home in Brockley. The Jamaican proprietor here took a motherly interest in me. At this time there were many more immigrants living locally and the club was a popular and much-needed refuge and social centre. It was here that men in drape jackets and baggy trousers would clutch me, and other girls, as we danced to ska and bluebeat. Pauline and Roy, Shirley and Lee and Johnny Ace. They would try to sweet-talk me into going out with them, but I always refused.

I loved children and often would babysit for the people in my area. There was an Irish family living across the road from the children's home where a friend and I spent many Saturday afternoons. The woman's sister used to wash and set my hair using only ordinary curling tongs, and no hot oils or pressing combs.

I also got to know other families from the Caribbean through some of the children I used to babysit and, consequently, young black men. This was how I met the man that I eventually married. Jane celebrated her thirteenth birthday the day we got married, and I think that it was probably also the first time she met him.

After my marriage I continued to work as a nurse, and when my children were small I always worked evenings or nights so that there were no babysitting problems – and when we did have rare night out, Jane would babysit for me.

My mother wrote regularly and we visited Birmingham once or twice. She had lost weight and looked frail but she did not seem to complain so much about her health and her sudden death came therefore as even more of a shock. One Sunday evening after the children were in bed I received a telephone call from one of my younger sisters: our mum had been in hospital for several days and had died that evening. She was 54. I learned later that the cause of death was heart failure as a result of anaemia which in turn had been caused by several long-standing treatable conditions. I thought sadly of all the years that she had complained about vague illnesses and how she had neglected to do anything about them.

I cried for a few minutes and then rang Jane. I did not go to the funeral. I looked after the children and Jane travelled to Birmingham to say goodbye.

3
Jane's Story

4 April 1949   B66 Stratford Road
                                             B'Ham 11

Dear Mrs Davidson,

Many thanks for your letter. Indeed it was a great shock
to me in so short a time. I do hope and pray the
Children have not taken it too badly. I have had a very
nice Rev. Gentleman to see me he said you asked him to
come. We had a word of prayer which did help me. He
came again Today and I did appreciate his coming. Well
Mrs Davidson I do not know how to tell you this but I
am placed very badly at the moment with regards to
money but I can straighten things out later on when I
have gone into everything. I will send £1.0.0. next week
and will arrange with you from then onwards. I am
thinking of going out to work to help things to be put
right. Could you help me by having baby Jane I would
rather her be with the Children, than put her in a
nursery she is a very dear baby. If it is possible I would
come down with my sister on Easter Saturday. I have a
good pram, also some nice clothes for her. Could you let
me know as soon as possible.

Yours faithfully,
Mrs McKenzie

Mrs McKenzie   8 April
B66 Stratford Road,
Birmingham, 11.

Dear Mrs McKenzie,

Thank you very much for your letter, which I was very
glad to have. It was not easy to break the news to the
children, which you may be sure that I did as gently as I
could. Sheilah [sic] took it to heart the most and cried
bitterly, but, naturally, being children they are all quite
cheerful and normal now and I know you would not
wish otherwise.

Now in regard to your baby. We should certainly like to
help you, but there are one or two important things I
must point out and would like you to fully understand.
To begin with, Jane would not be with the other
children to start with as our babies – all the under-fives –
are in the home in Brockley. They would be able to see
her sometimes but by no means every day. Then I am
not quite clear whether you mean us to take your little
ones permanently or only for a short time. We are
definitely not taking children in for short periods
however much we want to help parents. If in these
circumstances you still feel you would like to entrust
little Jane to our care we are willing to receive her.

We should certainly like to have the pram as we have not
a suitable one for an infant. You would need to get out
at St John's Station, which you pass through when
coming to Chislehurst. If you do decide to bring her I
can give you full particulars as to how to get there and
you can then fill in the necessary form. Please bring her
birth certificate, ration book and identity card. We shall
all love to see her. I am sure she is a lovely baby and I
feel for you deeply . . .

The Barbican Mission to the Jews

CHILDREN'S HOME

Agreement.

TO THE DIRECTOR.

DEAR SIR,

In consideration of your Mission having agreed to my request, and undertaken the charge of, and to provide for my child until

she   shall attain the age of sixteen years, or less as your Mission may determine; I hereby place under the guardianship of your Mission Jane Susan McKenzie born on the 10 day of the month of November, in the year 1948.

I agree to remove the child at any time you should call upon me to do so.

I agree, that whilst Jane Susan McKenzie is under the guardianship of your Mission, Jane Susan McKenzie shall, without discrimination or prejudice, receive Christian instruction, be brought up in the Christian faith, and be baptised at such a time as you think fit.

I agree, to pay regularly the sum of   per week towards the maintenance of the said child.

(Signature) _M__

Witness _____

....

Date .... 4 ....

It was 1949, four years after the war, when my mother travelled with me on her long journey from Birmingham to south-east London. She walked up the road from the station, pushing me in the pram. It was an early spring day, and there were buds on the trees. Behind the doors of the huge, four-storey houses we walked past, the upper-middle classes still lived the luxurious lives that they had always lived since the turn of the century, tended by servants. There was even the odd Rolls Royce.

Her emotions in turmoil, my mother approached the children's home and waited for the front door, panelled with stained glass, to swing open. Inside, and only a few steps across the black and white marble tiles, was another door through which she went into the dark hallway. The floor was lined with linoleum and the walls were painted dark green. The uncarpeted staircase had a polished wooden balustrade. She was greeted and taken into the staff sitting room, in which there were rugs on the floor, a glass-fronted bookcase stacked with Bibles, a large roll-top desk, a grandfather clock, ornaments on the mantelpiece above the fireplace and pictures of Jesus on the walls, one of which depicted a white Jesus, his arm encircling a group of children of different nationalities. This picture was a symbol of the work of the mission, drawing in people of Jewish origin from all over the world.

In this room my Jewish mother agreed a contract which signed away the next 16 years of my life and handed me over to another woman. The woman was called 'mother' too and was large and robust; but she was a different kind of mother – the matron to all the children in the home.

My mother left the large house having gained admittance at only one door, the door that led to the best room. It was used as a reception room, a visiting room and an office. She turned her back on the rest of the house and knew nothing of the conditions inside; even though she had reason to be wary after her experience with the municipal home in Birmingham. My mother left me at this house and did not return for ten years.

At the age of two I began to rebel, tugging at my curly hair and pulling chunks of it out. The doctor prescribed a long holiday with a member of staff to provide an opportunity for me to attach myself to one person. It worked: Auntie Nancy became special, and she was the one I looked to for warmth and understanding in the next few years. She was like a mother to me until she went away to get married when I was about ten and I never saw her again after that. I was not aware that I had brothers and sisters until the age of seven and, even then, I only saw them occasionally as they lived in the other part of the home in Chislehurst; and I cannot remember Thelma's visits to me, when she used to take me out, which she did until she left the home.

As time went on I began to wonder why my mother and father had both deserted me. I learned that my father had died when I was four months old, but I had no other information about him. My brothers and sisters sometimes received a parcel from home, and I always looked forward to receiving some small gift our mother had included for me, usually something to eat, but I relished whatever was given because I had very little of my own. When my sister and later my brothers returned home to our mother, the parcels stopped coming. I received an occasional letter with five shillings enclosed and a few words of recognition from my mother, but nothing else, and eventually even these stopped coming. Once I ran to the front door on my birthday where the postman gave me a card and although it was from my mother, I was sure it was from the postman himself: no one could convince me that my mother had remembered me on my birthday.

I grew into a young woman feeling that I was not her child. I became more and more disillusioned and my dream that one day I would return home as the others had done receded.

I was seven when I went home to my mother for my first

visit. It was at Christmas. I learned that she had remarried and had new children who lived at home with her. This made me even more unhappy: I had to return to the home and was not even given the opportunity to become part of her family.

Visiting day was always the first Saturday of the month, and even parents were not allowed to come on any other day. I had no visitors and, when the parents of other children arrived, I used to hide, feeling abandoned and resentful. Occasionally my friend Maureen and her sister would invite me along when their father took them out for the day. We usually went shopping in London's West End; I watched while he purchased their new clothes. We would eat sausage and egg and bacon and beans with tomato ketchup, in a café near Charing Cross station; I loved trying to get a bit of everything on to my fork so that I could taste it all in one go (in the home we had sausage or beans or bacon or egg, sometimes with a piece of fried bread, but never all in one go, all on the same plate).

Food and clothing were things we had to be grateful for, and we even sang songs to express that gratitude:

There is a happy land,
Far, far away,
Where we get bread and cheese three times a day.
Egg and bacon we never see,
We get sawdust in our tea,
And we are gradually fading away.

We were taught all about charity and love. The Bible was read to us after meals and we had no choice about our attendance at church and Sunday school. I sang 'Red and yellow, black and white, all are precious in his sight', and it made me feel included, but my feeling of being lost returned as we closed the chorus book.

After the day's outing with Maureen and her sister,

when their father had gone, I felt jealous of their gifts and new clothes. They were generous and shared their sweets with me, but this did not compensate for my longing for a father of my own. On one occasion I tore up Maureen's new coat, expecting to be severely punished – which meant getting the cane, missing all treats for a month or spending long hours alone in a room – but nothing happened. Nobody realised how upset this made me.

I was growing into an angry young girl, slamming doors and shouting to get attention. I did not talk much and tried to put thoughts and feelings about my father and mother behind me. I hated my mother, but wished secretly that she would come and take me home. She visited me once. I was ten years old and brought my new brother and sister with her. We went shopping to buy me a new coat; I wanted a duster coat because my friends had them. We couldn't find the one I wanted so instead she bought me a gingham dress. This was the only time my mother visited me and the only time she bought me something new: the smell of the new cotton has become imprinted on my mind.

The clothes I was used to wearing smelt of mothballs, as most were secondhand, sent to the home by wealthy families who no longer had a need for them. They were stored in a room at the top of the house, and every few months we were called one by one into this room to choose our clothes: I was one of the youngest and had to choose from the leavings of the older children. None the less, being able to choose made the clothes seem like new, and I considered myself to be well dressed, better, indeed, than the children who lived in the nearby St Michael's home. I rarely identified with other children in care whom I knew of or with whom I came into contact. However, when in school they sent a book with pictures of orphan babies in it round for us to choose from and pay a penny to Barnado's, I chose pictures of black babies and felt sad for them because their hair was shorn and untidy like mine.

We chose our shoes from the cubbyhole which was a

narrow passage at the side of the house with a glass roof and two doors like those in the conservatory. There were shoes of every size and shape, and most had been worn before. The room always smelt dank from the mildew which musted over the toes of the shoes and had to be wiped off before we could begin the process of selection. I had great difficulty finding shoes to fit my feet – they were already size fives at the age of 11. I solved the problem by wearing Thelma's moccasins when she had finished with them; at the age of 16 her feet were the same size as mine were at the age of 11, and I outgrew her later.

At primary school I learned to swim properly in a swimming pool in the new turquoise bathing suit my sister Thelma had bought for me, I was good at cartwheels and at jumping on a pogo stick. I learned my times tables and the art of absence from school without discovery. I read well but had no particular leaning towards books, and found comics boring once I had scanned the pictures; my time out of school was therefore spent listening to the same five or six gramophone records that we possessed and playing Monopoly.

On winter evenings I would sit with some of the other children around a coal fire, roasting chestnuts, and warming our bodies before we ventured into the unheated bedrooms for the night. On summer days I spent my time outside the house. We had only a small backyard which was usually full of washing, hung out to dry. Outside the back gate there were many things to amuse us: we teased the road sweeper about his 'kipper feet' and mimicked the girl down the road who could not talk properly. I began to notice that there were other black people in the area. The other children would say 'There goes your uncle,' calling my attention to every black man that walked past the gate; I would stare until he went out of sight, wondering about the disappearance of my father and his family. The children in the home and in the neighbourhood asked me questions about my parents. I knew nothing other than that my mum lived in Birmingham and that my dad was dead, and I answered as much.

Our leisure time was not restricted – as long as we had completed our chores and went to bed at the right time – and sometimes it seemed that we were left unsupervised for hours. The staff would disappear, and reappear at meal times, leaving us to seek them out if we needed something. Sometimes, just to make sure that we were not entirely on our own, one of us would stand at the bottom of the stairs and yell, 'Auntie Isobel!'

After a pause her voice would resound down from the top of the house, 'Yes?'

'Is a bell [Isobel] necessary on a bicycle?'

She never failed to respond to the urgent shout, no matter how many times we teased her.

I took the eleven plus examination, was graded as a borderline pass and given the opportunity to retake the examination in the form of an entrace test for a local grammar school. However, although I did not fail the second time either my name fell too low down the list to be accepted, and I ended up at King Alfred's School for Girls in Catford. It was there, in 1961, that I attached myself to a group of girls from the Caribbean. I spent the first few months being seen as a nice black girl by my white friends, while trying to qualify as a member of the black group. I was, however, a highly suspicious candidate with my light skin, and underwent rigorous questioning about my origins. I always replied airily, 'Oh, I'm a West Indian American', recalling snippets of what my sister Thelma had said to me about my father, and talk about an aunt on my mother's side, whom I had never met, who lived in America: I was proud to proclaim my allegiance to someone who was somewhere. In the end they would always want to know if I was a 'half-caste', and I learned that this was applied to me because I had a light skin and a white parent. Yes, I would say, I admit to being a 'half-caste'. I did not know whether or not I was supposed to be proud of this definition: it seemed like an important identification and therefore I stuck with it. The more information I could offer about who I was, and where I came from, the better chance I had of being accepted.

I made friends with Joy and Judith who became like sisters to me. I fell in love with the smell of cooking that wafted out as I climbed the steps to Joy's house, which was in the same road as the home. She would drop her keys down from the top floor of the house so I could let myself in, and by the time I had opened the door she would be down on the ground floor to meet me. She was often busy minding her baby brother and fixing food in the silver Dutch pot while her mother, whom she called 'Auntie' was out. We would talk about our plans to meet later to see the boys in the park while she went about her chores.

My friend Judy lived with her mother and baby sister in very different conditions: in her house there were many families, each one living in one or two rooms. Judy's family lived in one room and her mother cooked just oustide it at the top of the stairs: they had no kitchen, scullery or larder – just a cooker on the landing, and that they shared with the other people in the house. The room in which they lived was crowded with things, the bed was neatly covered with a candlewick bedspread, the dressing table was ornamented with pink crocheted swans, and the atmosphere was thick with the smell of paraffin from the heater, mingled with the scent of cosmetics. It was all right, I used to think to myself, at least they had a family – living in one room was better than having no family at all.

I kept up with my friends and excelled in most subjects including bad behaviour, although I managed to escape expulsion because I was a special case living in care. I was deeply disturbed when teachers cornered black pupils and told them not to behave as they did in Jamaica because they were now in Britain and must do as the British did. The white girls gossiped that my friends ate Kit-e-kat and took all the jobs. A girl in the home had called me a black monkey and I had beaten her with my leather strap. She went to the same school as me, with the other white girls in the home, but we were not friends and did not admit to knowing each other there.

I was not a great talker as we had no television or newspapers in the home and I knew little about current affairs and nothing about ordinary family life. I longed to have a father to talk about but I did not even know what he looked like; so I showed my friends a photo of Harry Belafonte which had come out of a chewing gum pack. I kept it in my wallet, and when I told them that this was my father they were kind to me and did not attempt to shatter my fairytale.

My new 'sisters' never came to the home: I had no family life to share with them and that was hard. I did not discuss my lack of parents and brothers and sisters with them; instead I learned about family life by being with them. I watched the way they dressed, imitated their hairstyles, learned to speak patois and to enjoy soul food.

There were a few years when, during the summer holidays, we went to camp in tents. A flurry of preparation preceded our departure by coach to Pevensey. We had to be measured for special camp clothes and then try on the dresses, socks, brown leather sandals, cardigans and navy raincoats from the piles of gear in store. Each item of clothing was then labelled with a name and packed into a kit bag, along with an enamel mug, dinner plate, pudding plate, knife, fork and spoon each – our property for the next three weeks.

We lived in white bell tents. We washed in the open air, using cold water in white enamel bowls. Our toilets were latrines dug by the big boys and shielded by canvas screens.

Every morning there was a military-style inspection: we had to roll up our straw-filled palliasses, pack our kit bags, lay everything neatly on our own groundsheet and be ready for the whistle. At the first whistle we hustled to line up in exact order of size behind our bed rolls, because when the second whistle blew we had to be standing to attention for the director to inspect us and our tent. The floor of the tent had been swept clean of straw, hair and cotton, the sides of the tent rolled up for ventilation.

'Any wet palliasses this morning?' the director would ask each day. The boys' tents always had wet beds.

Once a week both at camp and at the home the pocket money ritual was enacted. The director's wife sat beside a table loaded with bottles of sweets – dolly mixtures, jelly babies, pear drops, liquorice allsorts and treacle toffees. She held a Dorothy bag (a small soft drawstring bag) of pennies, threepenny bits, sixpences and, at one time, farthings and halfpennies. The youngest first, we all lined up to receive our money, and then we would 'buy' our sweets, 'spending' whatever amount we were allocated, giving the money back to the director's wife as she handed over the sweets.

We walked to the beach every day in pairs and returned for lunch at 1 pm. After lunch we played, visited Pevensey Castle or went for long walks. Three weeks of holiday and in my memory it never rained.

As the number of children in the home diminished, however, those camps stopped: the girls were sent off separately from the boys to camps run by the Christian Endeavour, held in an empty boarding school. Once Joy came with me and we had great fun: we were the only black girls and we pretended that we were sisters, wearing the same clothes every day and going everywhere together.

Returning to the home after the summer break was always difficult. I was one of the handful of children who did not spend the remainder of the summer break with my family. The house echoed with the emptiness. Most of the five or six beds in each room stayed neatly covered with a cotton counterpane. The linoleum shone, unscuffed by the usual number of children's feet, there was usually a fresh coat of paint somewhere in the house, and it was our job to keep the floors polished, taking it in turns to ride on the polisher that one of us would pull up and down the brown linoleum and finishing the job by wrapping dusters around our feet and sliding across the floor until it gleamed.

I first straightened my hair when I was 14. Thelma came to visit me and took me to see one of her friends, who was from Sierra Leone. Mrs Sandi used an iron comb which she plugged into an electrical socket, until it got very hot, burning my ears as she combed through my hair. At the end of the session my hair would look smooth, straight and shiny, and I was thrilled because I could comb my hair without hurting myself and make up new styles by putting rollers in it.

Thelma met Mrs Sandi because her three little boys would call out to Thelma as she passed their gate on the way to the home to visit me, and gradually we got to know the whole family. We sometimes ate there – traditional dishes served as communal meals on a huge plate in the middle of the table, and were regular visitors until they returned to Africa.

Thelma and I did not really *know* each other then. I was still at school and, although she had returned to London after living in Birmingham, we only met when she visited me at the home; and later when she was married we were still not 'close'. We did not talk about how I was doing at school and what I got up to with my friends; I did not tell her that I walked to school and saved my bus fare so that I could buy her and our mother a Christmas card; that when I stirred the Christmas pudding mixture, my wish was to be home with my mum and dad; she did not know that sometimes I was 'hopping the wag', missing school, to enjoy the social life I was not allowed at weekends.

At the age of 15, I started going to the local youth club. It was held in a school (coincidentally the one in which Tod later taught). I learned to dance to ska and bluebeat there and became attracted to smart-dressing black boys, some of whom were the younger brothers of the boys that Thelma knew. We did not live together; sometimes we did not even know what the other was doing – but we knew the same people.

I always had to leave the club before it closed because I was not allowed to stay out late in the evening. None the less it was here that I met my first boyfriend, who had recently arrived from Jamaica. I spent long hours dancing with him at the club and sometimes arrived home late. The punishment was being 'grounded' for a month, the cane or spending the remainder of the night in a downstairs room while everyone else was in bed. The latter was the worst punishment because I still believed – even then – that the only father I knew about – Father Christmas – would come down the chimney and get me.

As my sixteenth birthday drew nearer I spent long hours anticipating my release from the home. I had nowhere to go and the solution was to find myself a job as a nurse, partly because accommodation was provided and partly because my sister was one. I was too young to start training, but I became a cadet on a preliminary course, was offered a room in the nurses' quarters, and embarked on an independent life.

The next major event in my life was having a baby. I left nursing and stayed with Thelma for a while. She was married and already had children, and I began to learn about being a mother. I went to live with my boyfriend after that, in one room with a paraffin heater like my friend Judy and her family; I had lost contact with her by that time, as she – and Joy – had stayed on at school to take A levels.

I had no inclination to visit my mother until just before she died. She had written to me asking to see her grandchild and I had begun to feel a longing to see her, but I did not get there in time: soon after my nineteenth birthday she died.

I went to the funeral while Thelma stayed behind with the children. I was unaware of the pain holding her back, wanting only to see my mother for the last time. I travelled to Birmingham to join my other brothers and sisters, whom I had not seen for a long time and did not know at all well. We went as strangers together to the funeral. No one acknowledged me, or talked to me about our mother's life, her illness and her death. I had spent most of my life away from home and they did not see me as one of the family. No one recalled that I had only seen her three times since she had left me when I was a baby, or considered that I might wish to see her one last time and when I arrived the coffin had already been sealed.

I cried because I was angry and I was too late. I had been cheated. Her death came just when I had begun to yearn to see her and to ask her questions which had haunted me for years. I was furious at her burial: I felt nauseous at the thought of her body suffocated by the earth. And yet I wanted to blame her for bringing her black children into the world and then refusing to fulfil her role as a mother to them. She was young: only 54 years old. She did not stay around long enough to tell me about her love for my black father and her possible love for me. My thoughts and hopes about having the opportunity to gain her love went underground with her. Once again, and finally, she had deserted me. I was left without an understanding of why she had abandoned me as a child. And I had lost the chance to ask her about my father.

I feel that, by sending me away, our mother deprived herself of the comfort she could have derived from me, her baby, in her time of grief. My sister and I grew up away from her and a silence began to grow between all three of us, unspoken rules seemed to guard against any discussion about the life and death of my father. My sister and I did not speak to each other about either of our parents; and my father and my mother had maintained a silence of their own during their ten or more years together, so that little information about the relationship between our parents survived my mother, to be passed on to me by Thelma. My mother survived Ernest by 17 years. If I had only had the opportunity to talk to her, I might have learned so much more. At times I have hated her for her absence, and for the absence of answers.

4
Coming to Terms

Many years passed before we began to talk about these things. We were sisters but we scarcely knew each other, although we were doing sisterly things, like visiting each other. We may have passed on messages to each other from our brothers and sisters. We knew we had experiences to share, feelings about our own lives and circumstances to express but we did not know how to talk to each other, or to show how much we needed each other. As we grew up our feelings became like obligations: we needed contact with each other but the silence was always there. We look back on those women as though they were other people.

Back then Jane used to visit Thelma and spend time in her home after her marriage, playing records: bluebeat mostly, declarations of love, a search for something with which to identify. Music to make her feel good. She used to get so involved that she would spend the whole visit listening to the music, not saying a word.

At this time Thelma was busy being a housewife, and Jane watched the way Thelma loved and cared for her children, and, in this way, learned how to do the same for her own children. Thelma involved Jane in a practical family life, just as Elsie would have done, had the relationship existed. We were looking at and after each other, but about our parents we were silent, and there was a wealth of loss in that silence. Our mother had been surrounded by silence when our father died, and, for Jane, the silence began when she was sent into care as a baby.

All Jane had from our father was his name, the only thing – other than life – that he had given her. It was not, however, until the late 1970s, when Jane was in her thirties, that the silence and loss were breached, and it became increasingly important for her to discover her father and, at least, to search out the place where he had been buried. First, though, she wanted to find her mother's grave.

Jane

It was difficult. I took my friend Ebun with me to help me find the grave. She too had grown up without her parents. We did not know the way, and when we asked people for directions to Lodge Hill Cemetery they asked us 'Which Lodge Hill?' and we were sent all over the place before at last we found the right one.

My brother had told me that he knew the way to the grave, but not its number. I had spoken to the caretaker before and he, remembering my call, was very helpful. He asked me in what year my mother had died; I was unsure but recalled that it would have been in the late 1960s, a few months after my first daughter was born. He asked me whether I could remember the season of the year and, when I could not, thumbed through pages of names in the records book for about three quarters of the entries for 1968 but found nothing.

I began to apologise – it seemed ridiculous not to know the date of my mother's death or the location of her grave – but he was reassuring and I was comforted. I suggested that it could have been 1967 and he thumbed through again until, finally, he found someone named Elsie who had died on 12 September in that year. He told me details that I had not expected to be able to find out: my mother had been buried at 2 o'clock in the afternoon and the service had been conducted by a Reverend Beck. I had been at the funeral but I could not remember these details and they were important to me. He directed us to her grave and, when we found it, I was relieved to see her name on the stone, a solid confirmation for me in my search. I was sad, however, that my mother's grave was not tended, as many of the other graves were: the rose bush that I had been told had been planted was no longer there.

It was 20 years since she had died, and I stood by her grave feeling a sense of relief and of empathy with her. No one else in the world could have known what the experience meant to me: at least I felt at one with her. I knelt on the wet grass with tears of relief in my eyes. I wanted to pull up the earth and find out if she was still underneath; I wanted her back even though I had never really had her. Ebun was patient, saying little and standing back, not wanting to intrude, but as I became aware of her presence I no longer felt alone. She knelt on a plastic bag and said a prayer for me. It was a wet, windy day, one which I will always cherish and remember.

Finding my father then came to the fore: knowledge of him was an important part of me to which I could not get close. I began the search for his place of burial.

The family knew nothing. I telephoned the Birmingham Registry Office only to find that their records did not date back far enough. At their suggestion I investigated churches and private cemeteries, drawing a frustrating blank until I telephoned the Perry Barr Crematorium. The woman there warned me that it might take some time to search the records, but in the end it took no time at all: she rang back the next day to ask if my father's name was Ernest McKenzie-Mavinga.

My heart leapt. She said that he had been cremated there, and I was both elated and shocked. Just now it had seemed that my search would never end. I was 39 years old and I had only just found out that our father really did exist; I had even begun to wonder if he was still alive somewhere. However, when I asked her if there was anything I could visit, she told me there was no stone, that his name was in the records, but that was all. Wasn't there a plaque or marker that I could see as proof? No. There was only a plot where his ashes had been scattered and I could go there if I liked.

I was so disappointed. How unjust it was: no one had felt strongly enough about his life or death to mark it in some way; there was not even a grave or a stone to visit unlike our mother's grave. There was something tangible to mark her existence, but it was as if our father had never existed: I was enraged for a week about the way he had been treated.

Thelma

Adults sometimes forget that children need to grieve. They need to talk about the finality of death, they have to come to terms with not having been able to say goodbye, with what happens to a person's body, with having to share the grief of others. About 20 years ago I took my children to Birmingham to stay with my older sister Sheila and she wanted me to see where our mum was buried.

It was a glorious summer's day. We arrived to find that the caretaker had already locked up, but he was still around and understood that we needed to see the grave, and he allowed us to squeeze through the gap in the gate. We had to tell the children to be quiet, that it was not a park. It was a beautiful garden cemetery. A rose bush had been planted on her grave. It was beautiful and peaceful. (In the cemetery, my children decided: 'We are not gonna bury our mummy. We're gonna keep her body at home.' So I am going to be a hat stand.)

Our father died very suddenly. He went into a diabetic coma and developed pneumonia. He managed to hide his condition from our mother, and must have hidden any medication and looked after his own food, as she was apparently unaware that he was a diabetic. This seems to be just one indication of how secretive a man he was.

We grew up knowing nothing about him.

In 1979 we both became aware of a growing consciousness about our identity. It was a time of change both socially and politically for black people in Britain. Media attention focusing on the needs of young black children growing up in care stirred up our recollections of our experience in the home. We also began thinking about our experience of having one parent only, and that parent a white mother, and of our development and education as children without black role models.

We began talking about our parents' death, and realised that, although we had not grown up together, we did have some shared experiences.

We threw off the label of 'half-caste' and recognised that we were black women. 'Half-caste' is a term implying that half of us belongs to each race but that as a whole we belong to none, and as such, suspended in a racial, national limbo, have no place and no culture. 'Half-caste' has never meant white. By identifying ourselves as black women we were accepting the positive aspects of our African and Caribbean heritage, and starting to search for our personal history played a major part in that recognition.

Our awareness of the inequalities of opportunity in education for black children in Britain was reinforced as we realised the reluctance of the agencies concerned with childcare and education to include the black experience in the curriculum. We were bringing up our own children and knew that we had a contribution to make. Our studies as adults had shown that there was more to our history than we had been taught during our own education and upbringing.

We decided to uncover our father's history in order to pass it on to our own children who, although they had an advantage over us – they had fathers to grow up with – needed to realise the importance of knowing their family origins. Our research would mean that they would not be left with a legacy of silence.

Both of us were motivated to begin our search at the same time, but in different ways. For Jane, it was the television programme *Roots* which inspired her desire to 'belong', and turned it into a search, spurred on by the spectacular results of Alex Haley's own search for his family history.

Jane had inherited the name McKenzie-Mavinga from our father (Thelma used her married surname), but she had been taught as a child to drop the name Mavinga. Now she decided to start using her African surname and also changed her forename to Isha, a strengthening of her new identity.

In 1979 when her divorce was imminent, Isha's thoughts turned towards her family. Her husband's parents had emigrated long before, so there were no grandparents for her children, and it came home to her yet again that she was alone. Her fear of not being a part of anything, the legacy of the years in a children's home, returned, sharpened by the breakdown of her marriage. She yearned to belong to her own family.

By this time we were seeing a lot more of each other. Thelma, or Tod as everyone now called her, had become a mature student and had begun to study for a degree, for which she had to do an assignment. One of her tutors was curious about her mixed heritage, and suggested that Tod should write about how she, as a black woman, came to be living in south-east London. It was the beginning of an assignment that grew into a search for a history. Tod gathered a little material about our Jewish heritage, on our mother's side of the family, but we grew up and live in a predominantly white society which has dominated and confined us and, as Tod was able to discover very little material about our father, we chose to make our black identity the focus of our search. Why was there so little information about our father. We began to talk . . .

5
Yes, I Knew Your Father

It was 1980. Our two brothers were interested in what we wanted to do, but were not enthusiastic enough to do the research themselves. Andrew passed on some photographs of our father that he had been given by our mother before her death and, around the same time, some documents and letters came to Tod.

Some years previously the children's home in Chislehurst had closed after the death of the director. The mission had been taken over by another Christian organisation and all the papers relating to the children were sifted through, and sent to an ex-matron of the home who had kept in touch with some of the children. She gave Tod a manila folder which held letters that our father had written to the director of the home and his wife between 1943 and 1948, the last one shortly after Isha's (Jane's) birth. There were also letters from our mother, and the contracts that were signed when we were handed over to the home.

All this happened at just the right time. The letters gave us more to talk about and fuelled our resolve to continue our search. We began by writing some letters of our own, the first one to the heads of the social service departments of a number of city councils, in order to trace black senior citizens who might have known Ernest.

Our search continued at St Catherine's House where all the records of births, deaths and marriages in Britain are kept. We had a copy of our father's death certificate and our parents' marriage certificate. We also had a duplicate of our father's passport, issued by the Foreign Office when the original was reported lost. What we needed though was his birth certificate. St Catherine's House could not help us, so we made enquiries at the Trinidadian High Commission, and were told that, in order to get the birth certificate, we would have to know the parish in Trinidad where he was born, and then we had to enquire at The Red House (Trinidad's St Catherine's House) in the Trinidadian capital, Port of Spain. We were keen and needed to visit Trinidad ourselves, but at the time this did not seem possible.

By the end of 1981 we had tried every source of information we could think of, including writing to the leading newspapers in Trinidad; but there was no response. We even sent an appeal to Radio London's *Black Londoners* programme and the black broadcaster, Alex Pascall, encouraged us to keep trying, although nothing came of the appeal.

We even thought of writing to a masonic order. Our mother had once said that Ernest was the first black member of the Grand and Ancient Order of the Buffaloes. However, knowing the secrecy that surrounds masonic orders we were unsure of a response and decided not to follow up this particular lead.

For a few months we concentrated on our studies and our families. Then, in the autumn of 1982, we came across an article in our local newspaper about a man called Dr Ward, a Trinidadian, who had lived in Britain for over 30 years.

Charles Ward was born in Port of Spain, Trinidad. For 14 years he was involved in municipal politics, becoming deputy mayor of Port of Spain before he left Trinidad and settled in Britain in 1951. At the age of 71 he received his doctorate of education and, although he was retired he was still a freelance teacher lecturing on international affairs.

By coincidence we had a friend who was able to put us in

touch with him. We had tried contacting people across the world and here on our doorstep was a possible lead – someone who might have known Ernest. He lived in the same borough as us and we wasted no time in going to see him. He was very positive and promised to write a letter to his family in Trinidad, asking if anyone knew what had happened to the family of Ernest McKenzie-Mavinga.

Within weeks Dr Ward had a reply for us: he had a brother who had been a teacher in Trinidad and one of his old pupils was our older sister. Her name was Lynda, and she was the only surviving child of our father's first marriage.

The next step was to make contact. We wrote a cautious letter asking if she had any information about our father. We gave her only the barest details and waited anxiously for a reply.

It came at the end of June in 1983. We had never received post from Trinidad before so we were very excited. Lynda's letter confirmed that she was indeed our sister, and a living link with our past. With the letter was a piece of Lynda's sixtieth birthday cake, a copy of the order of service held to commemorate her birthday and some photographs of her family. She had received our letter when she had been recovering from influenza, and said she had nearly died of shock reading it, but was overjoyed to learn that she had a new family.

She also enclosed material about Ernest. There were two photographs and a photocopy of the headed writing paper used by our father at his office in London. The photographs were of delegates to the 1945 Pan African Conference in Manchester, and were similar to the ones that our brother Andrew had given us. One pictured all the Caribbean representatives who had attended the conference with their names listed below; the other was a close-up of our father taken at the same time.

We wanted to tell the whole world about our wonderful

discovery, but it meant little to anyone except us. Isha remembers crying for everyone that night: for herself, her sisters and brothers and for her mother and father.

Lynda told us that she was married with 10 children, 18 grandchildren and two great-grandchildren. At last we had our own extended family! We wrote back and exchanged more photographs. And then, in August, Lynda and her husband John came to visit us. Tod could not go to the airport, so Isha went alone.

Isha

Waiting for the arrival of the flight seemed to last a lifetime. Lynda was arriving with John, which added to my anxieties. I was about to meet two strangers. What would she be like? How would we find each other? What impact would this meeting have on the rest of my life?

The exit corridor seemed a mile long, there were people surging towards me and, suddenly, I saw her coming, my sister Lynda who I never knew before. I was aware of other people rushing towards their relatives and embracing them. But I could not do that. I walked cautiously towards her, kissed her and introduced myself. Then we embraced and began to talk. I could feel my throat beginning to tighten and the tears welling up inside. But I did not cry; just as I did as a child, I kept my tears inside, trying to find a private corner to cry in.

In our first conversation, as we made our way from the airport to my home, Lynda said that, for her, seeing me was a confirmation of Papa's death. For me, though, seeing her had brought him alive.

6
Lynda's Story

This is what Lynda told us. In 1916 Ernest Nicholas McKenzie, our father, married his first wife, Catherine Eugenia, and soon afterwards he was appointed to teach at a Roman Catholic school in Tobago.

Ernest was sent to Tobago as part of a policy to send newly appointed teachers to schools far from the capital, before allowing them to teach in Port of Spain. There were no government schools in Trinidad or Tobago: all schools were run by the churches – Roman Catholic, Anglican and Moravian (a Protestant sect). Tobago, like the other islands, was planted with sugar, the plantations covering almost the whole island. Most Tobagonians worked on these plantations and their children were Ernest's pupils.

Tobago was very different from the tourist resort it is now: many of the roads were tracks, and, when Ernest travelled to school by donkey, he had to ford a river because there was no bridge, a practice later blamed for his susceptibility to pneumonia. Some of Lynda's brothers and sisters were born here but they did not survive.

Catherine and Ernest returned to Port of Spain in Trinidad where Ernest began to teach at Nelson Street School, and in 1922 Lynda was born, the only one to survive out of Catherine's nine children.

She recalled that her papa was regarded as a skilled herbalist, as well as a teacher and storyteller who could enthral his friends with stories and jokes, needing only the invitation, 'Give us a joke Mr Mac', as encouragement.

However, Lynda could not remember much more about Ernest during this period because when she was seven years old, at the time of her first communion and confirmation, Ernest had already left for England, leaving teaching behind in the hope of becoming a playwright and furthering an interest in journalism. How she cried because her papa was not there to share two of the most important events in a Roman Catholic child's life. She did not see him again for many years, although they corresponded until she was 12, at which point he told her not to reply to his letters as he was going to Africa.

A year later her mother died and the event was reported in newspapers overseas in the hope that, wherever he was in the world, Ernest would read of her death. Lynda was looked after by her mother's relatives, and also had some contact with Ernest's sister and nephew. She also stayed in touch with her godmother's children who were like brothers to her. She remembers that once the eldest boy caught her playing with a doll and rebuked her, saying, 'You're too old to be playing with dollies now, you're a big girl.' Lynda put away her dolls: she was married within a few years.

During the early years of her marriage to John, Lynda believed that her father was in Africa, and hoped that he would return to be with her, especially as her mother was dead. One day in 1943, when the birth of her fourth child was imminent, she was visiting her mother's relatives. They were downstairs when they heard a knocking and calling at the front door above. Lynda climbed the stairs and to her amazement saw her father, Ernest, standing there. She flung her arms around him and had to call his name many times over to reassure herself that it was really her papa.

Ernest told her that he had been to Africa and that he had found what it was he had been searching for. He told her that his surname was now McKenzie-Mavinga, and that she had two brothers growing up in Britain, but did not mention Thelma who was by then a year old, nor did he say anything about his new wife.

Ernest remained in Trinidad for the birth and baptism of Lynda's fourth child and, when he left to return to Britain, Lynda felt that he was making preparations to return to Trinidad for good and to bring her brothers with him. It was not to be. He returned to Trinidad again, but always alone, and she saw him for the last time in 1945. She never heard from him again, even though she continued to write to his business address in New Compton Street for some years, and in 1949 she received a message from a Mr Chase, a friend of her father in Britain, who told her of Ernest's death and cremation.

Gradually Lynda lost contact with her own relatives in Trinidad and concentrated on mothering her growing family and caring for her husband, and for her mother-in-law who lived with them. Then in 1983 a friend was visiting Trinidad from London. He told Lynda he had heard an appeal on the radio from someone searching for information about their father, Ernest McKenzie-Mavinga, and later that year she received our letter asking about Ernest. The letter brought confirmation that he really was dead, but also that she had not only two brothers, but two sisters as well: Thelma, and Jane, who had been born several years after Ernest had returned to Britain.

Lynda grew up just like us, not knowing enough about her father. And, like us, she was so happy that at last she had a family of her own – the sisters and brothers that she had always wanted.

7
Going to Trinidad

The last few days that our new sister spent with us in London were spent in a whirl of shopping trips and visits. We went with her and John when they visited their friends, and discovered people who lived near to us and knew our sister and her family long before we did. Lynda and John found Trinidadian hospitality in Britain; and we got a foretaste of the welcome that we would receive in our father's country.

Lynda bought many little things: gifts for her children and grandchildren, mementoes of her visit and articles that were difficult to purchase back home, including some artificial flowers.

We took our families to the airport to see Lynda and John off. The airport was crowded with holidaymakers, but we were oblivious to them as we made our way towards the departure gate to say our goodbyes. Lynda clutched her bunches of flowers tearfully as she waved goodbye and disappeared through the gate. We looked down and saw a trail of plastic flowers that had slipped from the bunch. We knew that we were going to meet again soon. We gathered the fallen flowers and left the airport.

In February 1984 we were ready. We were going to meet our nieces and nephews, some of whom were older than us; those who had written to us over the past few months clearly enjoyed the novelty of writing 'Dear Auntie' at the top of their letters. Later they told us that although they had grown up with a lot of aunties and uncles, none of them were blood relatives, and now they had some real relations and were going to make the most of it.

Perhaps we would meet some of our father's contemporaries and hear more about him; perhaps there were older relatives who had known him too – already we knew that there was an older aunt who had helped to raise Lynda. We were doubtful about our reception, though; Lynda was wholly John's wife. She did everything for him and he expected her to do just that. Would her children be the same? We were independently minded women with our own views, and Trinidadian friends in Britain had often told us that the most chauvinistic men in the world were Trinidadian.

However, once we had made the decision to go, nothing was going to stop us, and we both spent days and nights trying to imagine what it would be like. There was much to consider and we asked advice from people who had been there. Should we take out insurance? What was the best currency to take. What should we take as presents? What essentials might be difficult to buy? Soap, underwear, chocolate and chewing gum, came the answer. Our resolve against taking too much luggage was defeated as the soft-sided cases began to bulge and smaller bags were pressed into use. We became overloaded carrier pigeons as we agreed to people's requests that we take this message, deliver that package, or carry a parcel for someone over there. And there was one important letter from one of our daughters: asking her Auntie Lynda to 'Look after mum and give her the time of her life.'

We left Britain on a cold clear February morning and, as our plane headed out across the Atlantic, we both felt a surge of joy. We were on our way to Trinidad, to see our sister again and meet our new black family. This journey was an essential part of the search for our history, and on it we were going to establish and reinforce our black identity.

We talked about what this journey meant to us, and recalled some childhood memories. What we had most wanted, when we were growing up, was to be part of a family. We recalled the times in Sunday school when we sang about 'Our Father in Heaven' and pointed skywards; and how the spiritual father we had learned about as children had not fulfilled our need for a real father. As the plane descended we began to feel apprehensive.

Piarco Airport was small and uncommercialised, the first floor balcony packed with people waiting to welcome the passengers. We felt as though they had all come to greet us, although there was no one there yet that we recognised. Immigration seemed to take so long. There were two queues: one was for returning nationals and the other for visitors. The queue for returning nationals moved a great deal faster than our queue, and a woman complained about how long it was taking to get through: 'This is going to take another hour,' she said; after having waited for over 35 years, another hour did not really matter to us. She had been there before, but this was our first visit.

Lynda and John and some of their children were waiting to greet us once we had collected our luggage and passed through customs. It was night and yet the heat enveloped us as we left the building, like having the door of a hot oven opened in our faces. We drove through the city towards Barataria, more concerned with renewing our relationship with our sister than with watching the city lights that were pointed out to us.

At home the rest of Lynda's family, our family, were waiting: our nieces and nephews and their children and their children's children. We were overwhelmed by the number of people at Lynda's house: family and friends had popped in to welcome us and we felt like very special people. At one point there was a power cut and the lights went out but the festivities continued. We both realised suddenly how we took electricity for granted – how a power cut in London would have disrupted the occasion while candles were sought, how we would have spent the following hour discussing the state of the electricity company.

Trinidad was very different from Britain. We were offered a fan to keep us cool during the night, where at home we would have been turning on the central heating. Our first few nights there passed restlessly. Everything, including the mosquitoes, was unfamiliar. All the windows in the house were open. We lay awake listening to the sounds outside, including a chain reaction of dogs barking throughout the neighbourhood, and remembered Britain where the tightly closed windows and double glazing block out the sound and the cold night air. At last we fell asleep to the sounds of the crickets and the tree frogs outside the window.

Our days were spent travelling around the island, trying to find out more about Ernest and the place where he had lived; and being shown off by Lynda, who wanted everyone to meet her new family. On each occasion, with each new person, we gleaned a little more information about our roots, and when we were alone together we talked about our reactions to what we had seen.

The houses, for example, ranged from large modern houses to bungalows to tiny ramshackle huts the size of garden sheds, perched precariously on tottering stilts – we wondered how people could live in them, and at the obvious wide discrepancy in living standards. The large brick houses, some standing in their own grounds surrounded by high fences and guarded by dogs, were a reminder of affluent times during the oil boom. The bungalows were sprawled amongst numerous fruit trees – mangos, guavas, limes, tamarinds, bananas and avocados.

We drove along smooth highways in constant traffic; in Port of Spain the rush hour lasted all day. The oil boom had resulted in a proliferation of cars; it was not uncommon for one household with several teenagers to possess an equal number of cars. It seemed to us that every adult in Trinidad drove a car.

Lynda wanted us to try as many Trinidadian foods as possible. We began the day with fresh coconut water and the jelly from inside the coconut and it became our morning drink. We had been told that bananas, guavas, breadfruit and pawpaw grew in Trinidad, but we were still amazed to see them growing in people's gardens, as we had thought they would only be found on plantations.

It took us a while to realise that we were in a black society. Everywhere we went there were black people who *belonged*: going about their daily lives, running businesses, banks and shops, managing hospitals, factories and the service industries. Trinidad had obviously progressed a great deal since Ernest had lived there; before independence, white people ran everything and the lighter the skin the higher the social prestige. People told us that if we had grown up in Trinidad we would have been socially more acceptable than our father because of our lighter skin colour. The sense of belonging we felt now was very important to us, as were the signs of power and status which black people had gained in Trinidad since independence.

One evening we went with the rest of the family to see the finals of a calypso competition. Artists like Sparrow, Crazy, Nelson, Brigo and Kitchener were appearing. There were some words and phrases we could not understand, and occasionally a member of the family had to translate for us so we could laugh along with them. Calypsos were originally the 'poor man's newspapers', discussing topical, political events, or the 'war' between the sexes in the form of song; some of the issues now sung about include apartheid, conservation and world peace. We were learning about carnival, our new family eager for us to share in and become part of Trinidadian culture.

We were invited to visit Santa Cruz primary school

where our niece Jasmine taught, and to take part in the junior mas', the part of carnival that belongs to children. The school was very overcrowded, with each room divided into two classes with children sharing three to a desk, and the day divided into shifts to accommodate them all. The children noticed our different accents and were curious, asking if we were tongue-tied! We wondered at the confidence they seemed to have in the teachers, the adults and themselves; a confidence that we as black children in Britain had never had, perhaps as a result of the sense of isolation as the only black children in our respective schools until the age of 11.

It was heartwarming to watch the children of all ages take part in the carnival, backed by the local steel band, and we felt very happy to be a part of carnival, which is so clearly a way of life and an integral part of Trinidadian culture.

Another aspect of the culture was the importance of sharing food with friends. Everywhere we went we were fêted with invitations to eat. There was crab souse from our nephew Terry; bus-up-shut (a kind of shredded roti or pancake) with crab and callaloo cooked by Lynda; breadfruit oil-down with baked fish when we visited Vilma, Lynda's adopted daughter; and curried lobster prepared by Lucille, an old family friend. At the home of another niece and her family we enjoyed an Indian meal which included channa, roti, curried mango and fried chicken. We feasted on shark with eddoes (a root vegetable like yams but smaller) and salt fish bulljhol (a dish including onions and tomatoes). On trips to the beach we had fry bake, corn bread and pilau rice, doubles (deep-fried batter dumplings stuffed with channa) and aloo pie. There were pastelles (a kind of dumpling made of grated corn, stuffed with meat, olives, raisins, and boiled in a banana leaf), freshly homemade coconut ice cream and an abundance of fresh fruits, and drinks made from them.

How Ernest must have missed the food and the con-
viviality. Food in wartime Britain was rationed and fruit
extremely scarce. People used to queue for hours for
anything fresh, whether it was oranges or cabbages. We
had grown up in a routine of bland meals served at the
same time, in the same way, every day. As adults we
learned from friends and in-laws how to cook food Caribbean style, and it was wonderful to sit around the table
discussing the various foods, how they differed from island
to island and how certain foods only grew on specific
islands.

Our visit to Trinidad to meet our new family was in-
strumental in the renewal of one of their family customs. A
few years prior to our visit they had stopped making trips
to the many beaches as an extended family occasion, but
because everyone wanted to share us and show us the
island we often left the city in a convoy of cars, each full of
adults and children, and several members of the family
remarked that they had forgotten how enjoyable these
outings were.

The family also took us to Tobago, Trinidad's neigh-
bouring island where, first of all, we did all the things that
tourists do. We took a boat from Pigeon Point, to view the
coral gardens and walk on Buccoo Reef; and we swam in
the 'Nylon pool', a shallow 'lake' of water, miles out in the
open sea. And then we got down to researching Ernest's
part of Tobago, where he had lived during his first job as a
teacher in a Roman Catholic school. Wherever we went,
our thoughts were with Ernest: we constantly asked questions and sought information about his and our past.

We were told about a prominent island family called
McKenzie-Bobb and we went to their house in Lambeau,
hoping to discover a family connection, but there was no
one at home. So we left a note on the gallery (verandah) but,
although a message acknowledging our note was left at the
hotel, we never got to meet the old lady or her daughter.

At Plymouth we questioned the rector of the local Anglican church, as there was no evidence that there had ever been a Roman Catholic community there, and he very kindly spoke to the oldest member of the little town on our behalf. But she was unable to recall a teacher called Ernest McKenzie.

We then visited Delaford, a community that was predominantly Roman Catholic. We knocked in vain on the door of the priest's house hoping to get a look at the school's records, but he was away. However, we found two men who had been at school there and although they could not recall a teacher with the name of McKenzie, they directed us to the home of Mrs Appleton, who was over 90 years old. Her family allowed us to spend a little time with her, but once again we were disappointed.

They in turn suggested that we visit Miss Orr, a retired teacher who lived in nearby Top Gully. But we had run out of time. Before we left the island we called at the government administration offices in the capital of Tobago, Scarborough. There it was suggested that we contact the head of the Roman Catholic Church both in Tobago and in Trinidad, which we did on our return to Britain. But our letters went unanswered.

Back in Trinidad itself, we spent a day searching through newspapers at The Red House archives, and visiting the teachers' centre and NJAC (National Joint Action Committee), an organisation concerned with the preservation of African culture in Trinidad, hoping to find some evidence of Ernest's writing and political involvement. We found nothing. Most of the people we visited were old men who had known and worked with our father but were unable to tell us very much about his early life and, of course, nothing about his life in Britain. They admired him because he had gone to Britain and, they thought, to Africa. He was said to have written books and articles but no one had copies of any of them. The school where he

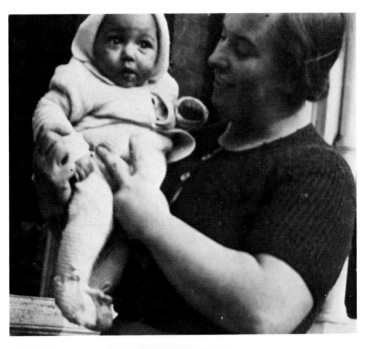

above
Thelma, with Auntie
Kathleen, when she
arrived at the home in
Chislehurst in February
1943

left
Jane with Auntie Evelyn
in the home in Brockley,
August 1949. This
auntie left soon
afterwards to become a
missionary

Mount Zion, the large home in Chislehurst which Thelma, Andrew, Teddy and Sheila went to in 1943

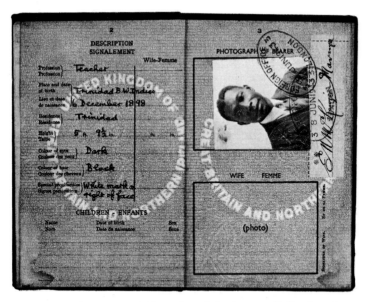

Ernest's second passport, which confirmed that he was tall, five feet nine inches, with white marks on his face, and that he had travelled to Trinidad several times during the Second World War

Our grandmother with her son-in-law Nathan and her grandchildren, our cousins Paul and Diane, in the back garden of their house in Selly Oak

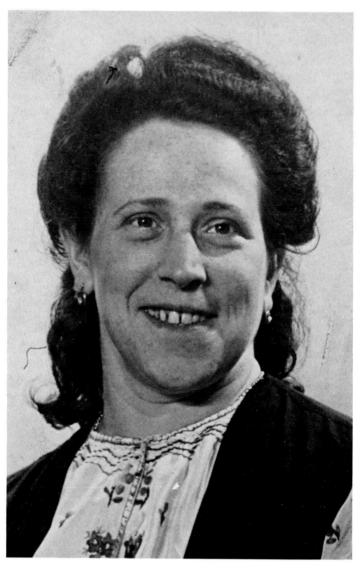

Our mother. The photograph was probably taken when she was in her early thirties, during the six-year gap between our births when she was healthy and relaxed

Our father, in a photograph which embodies the noble image recalled by
the people who had known him

The mission arranged for this photograph of Thelma (three years old) and her brothers to be taken

Jane aged about three with some of the girls that she grew up with in the home. We were never photographed together as a family

above
A snapshot taken on a visiting day of our mother with Thelma, Sheila, Andrew and Teddy in the garden at Mount Zion

left
Auntie Nancy, 'My favourite auntie', outside the home in Brockley with Jane and some of the other girls

left
Thelma as a teenager,
soon after she started
her first job in
Birmingham

below
'Wearing the new dress I
remember so vividly.'
Jane as a teenager

Lynda sent us these two photographs. This one was taken when she took her first communion and was confirmed at the age of seven years

Lynda as a teenager in Trinidad

This was one of the photographs which sparked off our curiosity about Ernest's political activity in Britain *Photo: Sunday Mercury, Birmingham*

NEGROES SEEK THEIR PART

The great desire of negroes is to take their share of responsibility in rebuilding the world, said Mr. McKenzie-Mavinga, secretary of the Caribbean Bureau, in Birmingham yesterday.

He was addressing a meeting organised by the Bureau to promote—as Mr. J. Silverman, M.P., who presided, said—better understanding between the white and negro races.

We found this article, which relates to the photograph, in an edition of the *Sunday Mercury* during our search at the Newspaper Library in Colindale

Ernest sent this photograph to Lynda soon after his arrival in Britain in 1930

This is a photograph of some of the delegates at the fifth Pan African Conference, October 1945. From left to right: Mrs Amy Garvey, Jamaica; Mr D M Harper, British Guyana; Ken Hill, Jamaica; Lushington, Trinidad; Ernest McKenzie-Mavinga, Trinidad; Gittens, Trinidad; P Williams, Barbados; Rojas, Trinidad; George Padmore, Africa Bureau

The plaque on the wall outside Chorlton town hall, Manchester, which commemorates the fifth Pan African Conference

THE CARIBBEAN BUREAU

E. McKENZIE – Mavinga

Secretary – Manager

Address : "CARIBO, LONDON

SECTIONS :

(a) PRESS AGENCY
Medium for the supply of
news to the Caribbean Press
and of the colonies to the
British People

(b) BUYERS FOR
SMALL TRADERS IN THE
CARIBBEAN COLONIES

(c) GENERAL INFORMATION
Medium for helping students
and other visitors from the
Caribbean Colonies to the
United Kingdom

ROOM 19

6, NEW COMPTON STREET
LONDON, W. 1
ENGLAND

A photocopy of the headed writing paper which Ernest used at his office –
another useful lead sent to us by Lynda

New Compton Street where we searched in vain for our father's office

1 October 1988. C L R James was the first person outside the family to confirm to us that he had known Ernest

Together   *Photo: Ian Perkins*

had taught – where one of these men had been the headmaster – had burned down, and therefore we could not even see the plaque that had borne his name and paid tribute to Ernest as a teacher.

Trinidad therefore produced very little for us in the way of evidence about Ernest's life. None the less, after our visit to Trinidad, we could visualise Ernest at 90, sitting with other old men on a gallery, drinking Vat 69 and being waited on by a long-suffering wife. All of these old men but John, our brother-in-law, were retired teachers or headmasters; and they all seemed to think that Ernest was marvellous.

They told us of their lives in the early years of the century: how they had walked the dirt tracks of Pitti Valley in their three-piece suits (there were no cars on the island then), going into Port of Spain at the weekend to 'lime' or hang out, and watch the girls go by in the heat, quenching their thirst with coconut water and rum punch, or by drinking water straight from the springs which tumbled down the rockside along the roads.

We were drawn into their memories, imagining Ernest sharing these experiences with his companions, and were sad only in that it was not our father recalling his youth for us, or perhaps telling us a bit about the history of the Trinidad that he knew and had learned about at school in St Joseph.

St Joseph, Trinidad's original capital, was founded in 1592, almost 100 years after Columbus had arrived in Trinidad. The first permanent settlement was established by Antonio de Berio, and was called San José de Oruna. Ernest's father was a cocoa plantation owner (probably because his grandfather had been given the land by his owner when he was freed). The planting of cocoa played a prominent part in the early colonisation of the island, and it was probably at St Joseph that some of the first plantations were established.

Our father's journey to school in the early years of the century would have been made on foot or on the back of a donkey. Children in those days were expected to greet politely any adult they passed on the way; if they neglected to do so they were in trouble: by the time they reached home the news of their transgression would have preceded them and they would be punished or severely scolded.

If rain came or there was a hurricane warning, children were expected to shelter wherever an adult offered a refuge. A message would be sent somehow to the anxious parents, telling them that their children were sheltering and safe. A hurricane warning did not necessarily mean that the island was about to be devastated; the island mountain ranges often ensured that hurricanes passed over and hit South America instead. But the islands are subject to tropical rainstorms, which can cause extensive flooding, and when Ernest was young, the floods were often catastrophic. Ernest would have seen the few roads and the tracks turn into floods as the water poured down the mountains causing the rivers to swell and overflow, and often he and his friends walked around the neighbour-hood ankle deep in water.

Ernest was, it seems, a carnival baby. The rainy season, late August to November, is a time when many babies are born. Nine months earlier it is the carnival season when, it is said, people lose their inhibitions during a brief period of celebration. Carnival baby or not, our Trinidadian grand-father was a respected member of the community, and Ernest was probably forbidden as a boy to join in with the carnival processions or even to watch them. His education and career were of primary importance and association with the carnival would have been beneath the family's dignity.

We continued to listen as the old men talked. They enjoyed recalling their youth and talking about themselves. They seemed to forget that we were there until we asked another question: what about schools in those days, the teaching, the equipment, the buildings, the discipline?

One of the men, Mr Burns, had actually been a pupil at Nelson Street School where our father eventually became the vice-principal. One of the largest boys' schools in the city, it had over 600 pupils, and consisted of one large room in which about ten classes sat in rows divided by age.

Discipline was very strict, teachers were in complete control, supported by prefects; pupils had no rights. Each day began with a roll call, which took place in silence and which set the pattern for the rest of the day. To break the silence was to break the rules, a punishable offence, and a leather strap was used to maintain discipline: if a boy spoke or was even seen by a prefect to move his lips he would be reported and then called out for punishment.

Ernest was in charge of roll call and was seen as a 'towering personality' responsible for discipline. He was not Mr Burns' teacher, but Mr Burns recalled him administering the strap to boys who misbehaved. He would hold the miscreant firmly by the back of the shirt collar while strapping the boy's buttocks. Among themselves the boys gave the teachers nicknames; they called Ernest 'Scald Jaw' because of a pink scar on the lower half of his face. The bravest boys would call out from the back of the class, and if they were caught the consequences were very painful.

To become a teacher at that time, a pupil usually became a 'prefect teacher' when he reached the age of 16. He would help the teacher by leading the other pupils in rote learning. The boys would repeat the lessons aloud, copy out script and take turns at reading passages. The next step would be the formal training, lasting several years with an examination at the end of each year. Once qualified, the teacher would be sent, as our father was, to an outlying school before teaching in a more central town or city.

Mr Burns left Nelson Street in 1925, when Ernest was still a teacher there. The next step in our father's career should have been to become principal of a school and retire behind a desk in an office, leaving someone else to administer punishment; although he would probably have had a long wait for a more senior position in a city school. Instead, he left for Britain to make a new start in life. He was still a young man. His interest in writing was evident – according to his old friends he was already contributing to various periodicals – and Britain seemed to offer him the chance to further this ambition. At the age of 29 he left behind his family, his friends, a secure occupation, his culture and the warmth of Trinidad, to take his chances in an unknown and very different country. From the warm breezes and welcoming rain cooling the earth in the dry season of the Caribbean Ernest came off the ship into the cold spring air, unprepared for the grey skies and clinging damp of Britain. Some of the men with whom we sat on that gallery had shared a similar experience on their arrival in Britain some years after Ernest. And they were glad to be back home.

Sitting there on that gallery with the sea in view on one side and the mountains on the other, Britain was far from our thoughts. We felt at home, relaxed and comfortable, listening to these recollections, and feeling as our father would have felt when family and friends came together.

All too soon the time came for us to leave Trinidad. First we had to go with our niece to have our ears pierced, as she had vowed that we could not leave until it had been done. So there we were, women in our late thirties, being taken by someone much younger than us, to have our ears pierced, which happens to most girls when they are babies. We felt it was her way of confirming that we were part of the family.

We felt emotional. We knew we had not had enough time. And we had really begun to feel at home with our newly found family. On the last night they prepared an exquisite meal and gathered round with gifts to say good-bye. There was a photograph session. We were loaded up with souvenirs for our families and plenty of food including black cake, tamarind balls, toolum and preserved mango. We left some personal belongings with Lynda, who was very sentimental and wanted to hold on to the memory of our visit.

We felt we had tasted a life which until now had been denied us, and we were leaving it behind; but when the plane took off, we felt no real anxiety. We had already made up our minds that we would return to Trinidad, and knew that this was the first of many visits to the home of our father.

Isha

When I was asked as a child, growing up in care, 'What do you want to do when you grow up?' I always replied that I just wanted a happy family.

When I arrived back in London my children were waiting, relieved that I had at last returned. I was bursting with news of Trinidad, overflowing with happiness; I had so much to tell and it all came bubbling out. They were very patient, although it must have seemed very strange – they had never seen me behave like an excited child before. For a short while in Trinidad I had enjoyed the luxury of being loved by a family, *my* family, and I felt like a child. It took a while to adapt to being a parent again.

We have telephoned Lynda several times and returned to visit Trinidad. She tells me again and again that I say things the way my father would have done. She is the only one who knows and who can tell me; without her I would not know this part of me – it is wonderful.

8
London

After that first visit we both knew that we had to return. Our mouths were watering with our first taste of the island and our family's culture. We could not imagine ever getting enough, and felt an empathy with the black people in Britain who feel that they must strive to keep on going back there. Part of our desire to return is a need to consolidate our newly discovered heritage, but we still feel we share the same emotion that compelled our father, and continues to compel other people, to keep returning.

We began to ask questions about our family here and in Trinidad, soon realising that we would have to find out the answers ourselves, as there were no immediate relatives to help us. Who, for example, could tell us why there was a six-year gap between our dates of birth, when our parents' first three children had arrived in quick succession?

Between the years 1943 and 1945 our father made several journeys to Trinidad. The evidence is in his passport and Lynda confirms that she last saw him in 1945. Our mother Elsie was then at home with four children, three of them under the age of three. For her, like many women at that time, family life was incomplete because her man was away from home. However, most women around her did have some support usually from their extended family; they were not bringing up black children and suffering isolation as a consequence.

We went into care in 1943 (Tod) and 1949 (Isha) during the last years of Ernest's life, so we began our search there and worked backwards from what we already knew.

We pieced together the fragments of information in our possession. From the amount of time that our mother was on her own, we supposed that our father was an inveterate traveller. Tod had been told by our mother that he had worked for the Ministry of Information during the war; we wondered whether it was political work that took him away from his family. The impression he gave our mother's relatives was of a cultured gentleman, someone who cared enough about our welfare to place us in a 'kind, Christian home'. To our sister in Trinidad he was a loving but absent father, a father who had left her to find his African roots.

We then considered the documents we had: his passport showed that he had added the name Mavinga to his surname in about 1942; but there was no evidence in the passport of a journey to Africa. There was the photograph of the Caribbean delegates at the fifth Pan African Conference held in Manchester in 1945, in which Ernest features along with eight other people: Mrs Amy Garvey (Jamaica), Mr D M Harper (British Guyana), Ken Hill (Jamaica), Lushington (Trinidad), Gittens (Trinidad), P Williams (Barbados), Rojas (Trinidad) and George Padmore (African Bureau). Some of the names were familiar, names of people who were prominent in the fight for equality and rights for black people at that time, people we had read about.

This was the sum of our knowledge about Ernest. We decided to use the photograph, our most tangible piece of evidence, as a point of departure. However, we soon discovered that the people we approached who had been part of the same political scene as him, or might have known people who were, were reluctant to talk to us about his life. Was it Ernest's involvement in politics, we wondered, that caused this reluctance? To his contemporaries, involvement in black politics may have seemed contradictory in a man who was married to a white woman, his marriage casting doubt on his commitment, even on his convictions. Why were people who knew him withholding information from us? Was their silence out of respect for a deceased comrade, or out of chauvinism?

We followed up every tiny clue, clutching at straws. We wrote to Ruth Prescott, after reading an article about her in *The Voice* which suggested that she might have been a friend of the Garveys. We enclosed the photograph of Ernest with Amy Garvey and the other Pan Africanists. This letter was one of our earliest attempts to obtain information. We received no reply.

We had not received replies to any of the earlier letters that we had written to the social services departments of city councils in Birmingham, Manchester, Liverpool, Leeds, Bristol and Cardiff, cities which had long-established black communities, and social clubs and venues founded and administered by members of the black community. We had asked the departments to pass on our letters of enquiry to any venues for black senior citizens.

We tried another tack and talked to people who had researched programmes for the BBC, and to other agencies concerned with the early settlement of black communities in British cities. However, most people we spoke to seemed unwilling to allow us access to their sources. The few who were willing to assist, though, were more than helpful. One, Peter Fryer, author of *Staying Power*, an extremely knowledgeable book on the history of black people in Britain, very kindly gave us several sources that he had used.

Dear Thelma Perkins,

Your letter of 25 February didn't reach me till yesterday, having been sent to Pluto's old address and therefore redirected twice.

Someone who might remember your father, or suggest other lines of enquiry you might follow is Peter Blackman, a Barbadian poet who has been in Britain since the 1930s and who edited *The Keys* in 1938–9. I haven't got his address, I'm afraid, but I dare say the Barbados High Commission might have it. (I used to have coffee occasionally with Peter Blackman when we were both working in the British Library Reading Room 40 years ago.) I take it you have already searched through the BL's file of *The Keys*? Did you also try under Caribbean Bureau, and your father's name, in the General Catalogue?

Have you tried the Black Cultural Archives? I gather that these are closed to the general public just now, but possibly an exception might be made for serious enquirers such as you and your sister. The person to ask about this, I think, is Len Garrison, at the Afro-Caribbean Education Resources Project in London.

You say your father used to speak at Hyde Park. A person who also did so (though somewhat later, I suppose), and may have some useful advice, is Roy Sawh, the Guyanese author of *From Where I Stand* (Hansib, 1987).

Many of the files of the old Ministry of Information are available at the Public Record Office in Kew. It may be that these include records of employees, though you might be in for a long and unrewarding search. The people on the enquiry desk there are very helpful indeed . . .

Slowly, a collage of Ernest's life in Britain began to emerge, forming a picture of a black man who was a father, a teacher, a journalist, a lecturer and a public speaker, a political activist and a businessman, with an office at No. 6, New Compton Street in central London.

This last piece of information came from Lynda who had sent us a photocopy of his writing paper, headed with the name of his business, the Caribbean Bureau, from which he apparently conducted his affairs as a shipping agent, a news agency and as a student liaison service. It was the first place that we decided to visit.

The office appeared to be the only contact address that the family in Trinidad had for him. At that time he had a home in Birmingham with a wife and family. He had a home, a daughter and, by then, grandchildren in Trinidad. We did not know, any of us, of each other's existence.

One spring morning in April 1988, armed with a street directory and the headed writing paper, we set off. We walked up and down Charing Cross Road in search of the entrance to New Compton Street, but to no avail; in its place was a new building, with a covered shopping arcade next to it. We walked through and found ourselves in New Compton Street. But we couldn't find No. 6. There was only the blank wall of a cinema. A sense of dismay and disappointment descended. We hadn't let on to each other how much we had hoped to find some sign that he had been there, an office building or a door with business plates, one with our father's or the business name on, perhaps. If the building had still been there, we could have gone in; we had both envisaged stepping back into the forties and retracing our father's steps upwards, along a corridor into his old office. We walked up and down the road looking for No. 6, trying to decide what to do next. Eventually, we walked back through the shopping arcade and into a long-established London dance footwear shop.

We asked to speak to someone who had been working in the shop for a long time, in the hope that they might recall the original street and its buildings. A friendly woman appeared from the back of the shop who did. She said they had been demolished after the war. It was all she could tell us but at least we knew that the place had existed. We realised that disappointment would be a constant companion on our search.

Ernest's office in New Compton Street had been his base during the war years and up to his death. The cache of

54,Claremont Road,
Birmingham,I9,
3rd February I943.

5 FEB 1943

Rev.I.E.Davidson,M.A.
    Director,B.M.Mission to the Jews,
        Mount Zion,
            Lubock Road,
                Chiselhurst,Kent

Dear Reverend Davidson,
        This is to acknowledge the receipt of your telegram
of Friday last to which I have replied and your letter dated
Ist instant.I have to thank you very much for both and to
assure you how much I appreciate your promptness in respond-
ing to my request.As I said in my letter,although the
colour bar exists in this country (very callously too) yet
I am confident that with true christian in practice there
can be no colour discrimination. I can forsee that,when the
time comes forrsettling the peace if christianity be not
allowed to play the major part in the reconstruction of
the world,the next war will be swift in coming and even
more disastrous than this one.
        Coming to my reply,I sent to say that the
children will be brought in on Saturday next.I could not
reply before as I was at Leicester when the telegram
arrived.As I shall have to be out doing some work on
Saturday,I have asked the mother to take them in.I shall
try to make it convenient to travel into london within a
fortnight from Saturday next. I expect that they will arrive
about mid-day.Any documents to sign may be sent on to me.
I shall sign before a credible witness.
        Regarding payment for the upkeep of the
children,I want to say that,although the Government asked
me to take a training course at Leicester when I arrived
there last Friday,I was told that no arrangements were made
as yet by the Central Birmingham Exchange.It would appear
that the colour bar is doing its fell work again.I have
selected draughting as I know that work already,so that
the course to me would only be a refresher one.But that
course would entitle me to office work---that which the
industrialists are now refusing to give me on account of
complexion.For this reason,I believe difficulties will
arise.However,I do a little work on my own.That has been
helping me to keep the wolf from the door.I shall be prepared
to apy regularly your charges.But do,make them the minimum.
During this season takings are usually very lean.
        In my last,I told you the real reason
why my wife would part with the children.She is affecting
that she is not feeling helathy enough to take care of
them½ I should like you therefore,not to mention anything
about her family prejudice when dealing with her.I am
remitting five shillings (5/-) which I trust would indemnify
you for the cost of the telegram.
            Again thanking you,
                I remain,
                    E.M.McKenzie

letters which had come to us after the death of the director of the children's home filled in more detail about his business, his travels around Britain and his experiences as a black professional.

One letter details how, in January 1943, he prepared to travel to Leicester, to study draughtsmanship. His place on the course had been secured with the help of the Colonial Office, but when he arrived in Leicester, there was no place for him, no arrangements had been made. He blamed the colour bar, an obstacle he had often come up against while trying to get work or training in the areas of his interests.

Black men in Britain then suffered considerable financial hardship and had to try all manner of ways to support themselves and, in Ernest's case, a family. The various jobs to which Ernest turned his hand, apart from his work at the Caribbean Bureau, included running restaurants and clubs, peddling herbal remedies around the country and telling fortunes as a 'kai' showman, and even appearing as an extra in films which needed Africans in crowd scenes. Ernest, like several of his friends, was an extra in the film *Sanders of the River*, which featured the black American actor and singer Paul Robeson. Circumstance as well as ideology drew these black men together to support each other and voice their feelings. We began to try and seek out some of the men, or their relatives, who may have been working in Britain in the same situation at the same time as Ernest, as the next stage in our quest.

Sam, a Trinidadian known in political circles as Eli Shabaz, was the first man we met (Shabaz was one of Malcolm X's names). Sam, in conjunction with Sam Uriah Morris, was a founder member of the National Institute of Black Studies, and was involved in the African liberation movement in the sixties, the Universal Coloured Peoples' Association and in the Black Panther movement. More recently he has been working with Hackney Black Peoples' Association. He has, throughout his life, promoted the study of the history of

African civilisations, and his enthusiasm about our book was evident. His close links with the black community in Britain and his knowledge of Caribbean culture informed our search and reinforced our commitment to the postiveness of being black. We felt that he was encouraging us in the excavation of our heritage in the same way that our father would have done.

One of the contacts which Sam provided us with proved to be very fruitful. For some time we had been trying to get an interview with C L R James, one of the Caribbean's most eminent writers and political theorists, who had also been associated closely with the struggle for black consciousness in Britain. But he was very old and the people closest to him were understandably protective of him. Sam gave us a contact telephone number and we were, at last, able to make an appointment to meet the writer and historian.

Saturday morning, 1 October 1988, was warm and bright. We set out for Brixton in south London. Mr James' personal assistant welcomed us and took us to meet C L R. He sat, surrounded by books, all four walls lined from floor to ceiling with shelves. We were oblivious to the noise of the traffic passing below and to the comings and goings elsewhere in that busy house, our attention focused only on the feeling that this was probably what talking to our father would have been like, had he survived to be 90 years old.

Mr James recognised our father from the photograph that we showed him. He told us that Ernest had been asked to attend the 1945 Pan African Conference as a Trinidadian delegate. He remembered him as a figure of authority, who sat and directed while the younger men did the running around. C L R asked us if we knew our father had been a preacher; we told him that our mother had mentioned that he used to speak at Hyde Park Corner. C L R recalled that Ernest used to begin by talking about God, but that religion was not his central theme: he was more concerned with the plight of common people and with his brand of socialism.

C L R had known our father as a political activist, and suggested that the office in London was probably a meeting place as well, where people left messages, booked tickets for travelling and dealt with correspondence for various causes. He also confirmed that, as relatives and friends had told us, our father had been an educated man, who could speak several languages, including French, Spanish, Russian and one or two African languages.

C L R was the first 'outsider' to affirm for us that we were on the right track and, like Sam, he was enthusiastic about our project. He encouraged us to contact Lord Pitt, Britain's first black peer, whom he thought might also be an important source of information. We had already tried once to talk to Lord Pitt but had no success; now we resolved to try again. C L R also suggested other places and people that might help, and we were elated when we bade him goodbye. The first of October was a landmark for us: after eight years it seemed as though things were finally coming together.

One Sunday soon after our visit to C L R we set off to meet one of the people he had suggested we see, Mrs Sarah Busby, who had first come to Britain before the Second World War. We were made to feel very welcome but she was not able to give us any information about Ernest. Her family was interested in our project and offered more suggestions, reiterating the idea of persevering with Lord Pitt. They also suggested that if Ernest had had any written work published in Britain, we would find some evidence in the British Library, particularly in the newspaper coverage of the Pan African Conference held in 1945.

October 1988 proved busy and momentous. We continued to write letters to contacts in Edinburgh, London, Jamaica and Trinidad. We questioned anyone close to us who had met or known our father. Our aunt Bella, the sister who had been closest to our mother, was able to give us snippets that recalled our mother's life with Ernest and her own impressions of her brother-in-law; however, she died at the end of that month and her death reminded us of the time factor: the people that we needed to interview were almost all senior citizens, and most were over 80 years old.

We spent a Saturday morning at the British Library. People had told us that our father was a published author. In Trinidad, Lynda told us that the last time our father had been home in 1945, he had been something of a celebrity; she remembers that his autobiography had just been published and that his name was added to his old school's roll of honour. We have never seen a copy of this book; perhaps his own copy was buried in the rubble when the house in Birmingham collapsed. We have searched in several libraries for it, including those of the University of the West Indies, and there is no sign that it was ever published. Lynda also said that one of his letters mentioned a play he had written and that it had been performed: he had said that she must see it should it ever reach Trinidad. Our mother had also told us that Ernest had written for radio and for periodicals.

We searched in the catalogues for the name McKenzie and checked all the variations: Mckenzie; McKenzie-Mavinga; MacKenzie; Kenzie. (After emancipation, freed slaves needed surnames to own property, marry, travel, or carry on a business. They had been forced to discard their African names on arrival in the Caribbean and had been given 'Christian' names by the plantation owners. Once free, they tended to adopt the surname of the person to whom they had previously belonged. There is a predominance of surnames of Scottish origin in Trinidad, suggesting the nationality of many of the plantation owners. Our grandfather, Joseph McKenzie, must have inherited the surname that had been adopted by his father who had probably been a slave; but had our great-great-grandfather's name been Mavinga, we wondered. And what part of Africa had it originated from?) We found nothing under any of the names.

Disappointed, we wanted to search further, to find *something*. We found a reference to a book about the Pan African Congress and went through the procedure of reserving it and becoming temporary members, which allowed us into the reading room, where we settled down to read *First Pan African Conference on Pre-History*, edited by L S B Leakey, published in 1947.

The names and dates in the book were unfamiliar; our father had not been a contributor; there were no references to him. The book was an account of a conference on anthropological and archaeological research! We spent about two hours on the preliminaries involved in getting hold of, and two minutes reading a book we did not want.

However, while we were at the British Library, a helpful member of staff suggested that we go to the Newspaper Library at Colindale. On the long journey across London we had time to dampen our expectations; after the disappointment at the British Library we did not hope to find anything.

First we checked the index, using our photographs as a guide. The Pan African Conference had been held from 13–21 October 1945 in Manchester; so we selected the *Manchester Guardian* for scrutiny. On the back of one of our photographs was the rubber stamp of the *Birmingham Mercury*, a long-established weekly newspaper. We were unsure of the year in which the photograph had been taken, so we decided to look at the newspapers between 1945–8. Judging from the photograph, it was probably taken in winter: most of the people in it were wearing warm coats and hats, and our father was wearing a scarf.

Once we had mastered the machinery and began viewing the microfilmed pages of the *Manchester Guardian*, our pessimism was dispelled. As soon as we came across the first article dated 14 October, on the opening of the conference, we began to feel excited. 200 delegates representing the 'coloured' world had attended the opening of the conference held at Chorlton town hall. A second report made reference to Marcus Garvey's widow Amy, who appeared in the photograph with our father; on 16 October, she addressed the conference calling for solidarity in the struggle for black freedom.

The previous day the conference had discussed the 'coloured problem in Europe', delegates having expressed freely their opinions on the subject of discrimination against 'coloured' people. One Mr Richardson who had lived in Manchester for 45 years, declared that he intended to stay and help 'civilise' the British people; other speakers stressed the sacrifices made by 'coloured' people in fighting the war for liberation. A Ghanaian speaker, Mr Appiah, was reported as saying, 'It is only force that will bring us out of this disgraceful condition in which we find ourselves.' And Mr Jomo Kenyatta, later to become the first president of independent Kenya, called for an act of parliament outlawing discrimination. That was in 1945; it was almost 30 years later that the Race Relations Act became law.

On 20 October the conference passed a resolution demanding equal opportunities for all children born in Britain, and that discrimination on the grounds of colour and creed be deemed a criminal offence. We were impressed: we did not know that the movement for equal opportunities started so early in this country, nor that our father had been part of it, he and his contemporaries together campaigning for their British-born children.

The newspaper reported on the events of the last day of the conference and the closing speech made on 22 October, by Dr W E B DuBois, journalist, social scientist, historian and leader of the black struggle in the United States, summarised the history of the Pan African movement for the delegates, and vigorously attacked 'The crazy idea of the white people of Europe that they should run the world.' Instead he advocated a world organisation which would reach out to all groups of coloured people, and 'beat back the organisation of lies which marks the coloured man wherever and whenever he attempts to better his condition.'

We were very satisfied with the discovery of such positive evidence to link in to one of our photographs. Now, however, we had five volumes of the *Birmingham Mercury* to look through. During three hours of scanning we learned quite a bit about life in postwar Britain, particularly in Birmingham.

The newspaper referred to black people as 'coloured', a word which today many regard as an insult, but which at that time was seen as being polite. Children of mixed race were known as 'half-caste', and one column, accompanied by photographs, spoke of 'khaki-coloured woolly-headed children'. The *Birmingham Mercury*, in 1945, reported on the number of such children in care and the difficulty of finding suitable foster parents. The illustration showed a woman of mixed race, who was fostering several children, black and white, doing the hair of a white child, with a child of mixed race standing beside her. This was quite an insight into the climate of opinion in which our mother had been expected to bring us up, and we speculated about the impact that it may have had on our father.

Although these snippets were helpful to our research they tended to slow us down, until suddenly we saw *it*. An article with Ernest's name in it, in the *Sunday Mercury* of 24 November 1946. We exclaimed, oblivious of everyone around us, and of the hushed silence in the reading room. There he was in print, featured in a story about a meeting arranged by his own Caribbean Bureau to help build understanding between the races. We were elated, our hopes confirmed, at long last here was a positive return for all the energies we had devoted to this project.

We were grinning widely when we left the building; we couldn't stop grinning or talking about our find. After eight years, we had come such a long way in only a few months. However, we were a little disappointed: we had not found any mention of Ernest in the press coverage of the Manchester meeting which would underpin C L R James' recollections.

Of the delegates who attended the conference, 33 represented the Caribbean. Our father had been visiting Trinidad just before the conference and, as he was a member of the West Indies National Party of Trinidad, he, and a fellow member, Lushington, were elected to represent the party at the conference.

Our father was regarded as a brilliant speaker, whose eloquence electrified audiences and impressed many people including David Pitt (later Lord Pitt), as we discovered when, encouraged by C L R James, we made another attempt to contact the peer and received a letter from him, in which he wrote that both Ernest and his colleague had given a good account of themselves at the conference, and that he had known Ernest in Trinidad, but he could remember little more.

Our research into Ernest's involvement in the Pan African movement meant that we were able to piece and link together the personal and political aspects of his life. Between 1900 and 1945 the Pan African movement grew rapidly and gathered support for its promotion of positive black self-identity; a process which must often have mirrored Ernest's own experience, as he became part of a growing, supportive political network dedicated to his advancement, his future, and the future of his black children. Evidence suggests that one of our father's aims was to take his children back to Trinidad, the land that he knew and loved, and his concern about our cultural and racial needs and future makes us feel an empathy with that movement, and take pride in our efforts many years later to learn about it and him.

In his letter, Peter Fryer had advised us to return to the British Library and have a look at copies of *The Keys*, the journal produced by the League of Coloured Peoples, as he thought it possible that Ernest may have contributed to the journal.

We returned to the British Library and during April 1990 we spent two mornings there researching *The Keys*, in the course of which we came across many of the men who had campaigned against the colour bar during this century. There was Harold Moody, a Jamaican who had studied medicine at King's College in 1904 and encountered racial discrimination both in his search for accommodation and, as Peter Fryer's research shows, in his efforts to establish his career. He had qualified as a doctor but was not allowed to take up an appointment in the hospital because the matron refused to have him there; and he was also rejected for the post of medical officer for the people of Camberwell because he was a 'nigger'. However, the poor people just down the road from Camberwell came to appreciate their local doctor, when he set up his own practice in Peckham in 1913.

Students like Dr Moody had been encouraged to come from the colonies to study in Britain, often at great expense to their families. But they experienced discrimination to such an extent that the Colonial Office was forced to acquire and open hostels to accommodate them. Landlords refused to let rooms to coloured students and went so far as to include clauses in tenancy agreements forbidding tenants to sub-let to coloured people. The League of Coloured Peoples itself kept a list of boarding houses that were open to people from the colonies.

Dr Moody was a founder member of the League of Coloured Peoples, a moderate organisation with 12 centres in Britain, which campaigned for social acceptance and equal rights for black people living in Britain, and for anti-racist legislation. Its motto ran:

The League exists to promote and protect its members' interests. To interest members in all coloured people, to improve relations between the races, to co-operate with kindred organisations, to assist financially where possible.

Although the Church of England condemned racism, a member of the League who found racism within it was Peter Blackman who had come to Britain from Barbados to study theology. According to Peter Fryer, his first posting was to West Africa where he experienced such racism from the colonial establishment that he decided to leave the church and return to Britain. Blackman was the leader of another organisation, the Negro Welfare Association, he was also editor of *The Keys* from 1938 to 1939, and, like Ernest, was a socialist.

Black intellectuals found, as our father had, that the establishment was not keen that they should better themselves in Britain. George Padmore, born in Trinidad, came to London from Moscow in 1925. He was an ardent Pan Africanist and while championing the cause for the liberation and advancement of colonial Africa, worked as a teacher and journalist. He was also a great friend of C L R James, who had lived in Britain for six years between 1932 and 1938 before going to America.

Ras Makonnen was another Pan Africanist who hailed from Guyana. He studied at Manchester University and later started a chain of restaurants in Lancashire which became social centres for black people of all nationalities during the Second World War. Some of the profits from his ventures were used to help finance the fifth Pan African Congress.

One of Trinidad's most famous cricketers was also in Britain during this period: Learie Constantine lived with his family in Lancashire and, during the war, worked as a civil servant; yet while on business in London he and his wife were refused pre-booked hotel accommodation on the grounds that he was a 'nigger'.

Our hunt through *The Keys* proved worthwhile, and not only in gathering information about Ernest's contemporaries. On the second morning in the north gallery, we went through the issues dating from 1930 to 1950, some of which were in very poor condition and extremely fragile. Towards the end of the morning, in one of those issues marked 'fragile', we saw the name E N McKenzie among the list of contributors, and felt the same explosion of euphoria all over again.

It was in the 1934 winter issue, and the article was entitled 'What is the Ethopian's [sic] sin?'. He began by discussing the religious aspects of unity and continued by saying that although the League of Coloured Peoples has many well-intentioned white patrons and members, not enough coloured people supported the group or other groups with similar causes. For groups to be effective, he argued, they must have the support of their own kind.

What is the Ethopian's Sin?

By E. N. McKENZIE

The Jews crucified Christ, for playing their part in the plan of the creation they have, for a protracted period, suffered ostracism by the so-called Christian world. True it is that the ancient glory of Ethiopia hath departed from her, and during the course of that evolution through which every race must go, the Africans reverted into primitiveness. The same may be said of the people for whom Confucius exercised his brains; the Arabs for whom Duraid ibn al-Gimmah and Saladin wrote and fought. But unlike the wily Mongolian and the fierce Arab, the African simply degenerated (if it should be called degeneration) from a civilised entity into a bush-man. Yet in that state, Africa has preserved a code of moral laws whose tenets make better provisions for the chastity of her children, and are more strictly observed than any Christian precepts by christian people.

Semitics and Mongols alike are tolerated (mark well, not appreciated) whilst the treatment meted out to coloured people, in some instances, is nothing short of persecution.

Is it because, in the simplicity of their nature, the Africans allowed themselves to be wheeled, stolen and enslaved three hundred years ago? No, it may not be, for, they did not sin, somebody sinned against them then. Besides, their Saxon brethren cannot deride them for that misfortune. They passed through the same drill before. There is a trail of human nature which causes an individual either to suspect or admire the brother who makes phenomenal advancement, particularly when he does so in the face of difficulties. A century is a short period! Within that space the coloured man, with his characteristic aptitude to assimilate what is aesthetic has found himself fighting for social equality in the world. He is not, and cannot be satisfied with toleration after his schoolmaster–the white man–has taught him the difference between a palace and a hovel, a difference which he appreciates. The schoolmaster ought to be proud of his pupil. The emancipators ought to feel gratified that the emancipatees' advancement has justified any sacrifice they may have made. But instead a prejudicial barrier is raised. There must be a reason. The Ethiopian's aim is the reason. What is that sin? This is the answer: the average coloured man wants to be appreciated as an individual, whilst he refuses to appreciate the work of his own people. He seeks to set a standard of value on himself alone and thereby flouts his brother's work. This fosters a lack of cohesion among the members of the race. There is no greater example of this disunited spirit than the scant support given such an organisation as the League of Coloured Peoples by coloured people in the United Kingdom. This is a belief–a well founded belief–that there is no innate apathy on the part of the white people for the coloured people. This is manifested by the interest that some highly placed English people take in the League. Every act of prejudice exhibited by any white person against a coloured man should enerve him to so conduct himself, that his white brother would realise to his shame, that Cowper did not make a mistake when he wrote:

> "Fleecy locks and dark complexion
> Do not forfeit nature's claim.
> Skins may differ, but affection
> Dwells in white and black the same.

We learned later that this article arose out of a very specific experience. Ernest had visited Liverpool several times and had been upset by the level of racism experienced by the black community there. He decided to open a restaurant and club as a meeting point, where people could discuss the issues involved and share experiences. However, his customers took advantage of his generosity; although they used the place to sit and talk, many of them did not pay for the food they ate, and Ernest was left with the bills and running costs. The venture did not last very long and he returned to London, bitter and disillusioned. He knew several well-to-do white people there who were interested in the political dilemma facing black people. One of them, Mrs Malcomson, who was a Quaker, talked the restaurant experience over with him and helped him to realise that positive and negative human qualities were independent of race.

He became a member of the committee of Stanley House, a centre in Liverpool opened by Sir Henry Morton and Lady Stanley for the use of the black community. This necessitated his travelling to Liverpool frequently, and he overcame his bitterness and concerned himself with the political attitude of black people, writing the article in *The Keys* after some discussion with an associate.

One issue that all the various groups were united about was the treatment of the black members of the armed forces. It was only through the efforts of Dr Harold Moody and his associates that black people in the forces during the Second World War actually became eligible for commissions. Black members of the forces were not only subject to discrimination in promotion, but they also suffered segregation in the mess halls and in the hospitals. In some cases a screen was used to divide the mess hall: the black servicemen had to wait until the white servicemen had been served before collecting their food and then retiring to the hidden section of the room to consume it. It was a white member of the airforce who discovered this anomaly and wrote of it to *The Keys*. He had challenged his commanding officer about the situation and was told, 'They have not learned to behave like us'. The writer of the letter then asked how much learning one needed to drink a cup of tea and eat a few slices of bread?

The Keys reported another incident that reflected the racist attitudes of those in command in the armed forces. A young white woman attempted on three successive days to visit some wounded black airmen in the hospital at RAF Tangmere, but was turned away each time. The officer who refused her admission was said to have expressed his personal view that, by visiting 'coloured' men she was lowering the prestige of white people. He was talking about men who were fighting and might die for Britain, men like our father, and many other black people in Britain at that time, who helped rescue and care for people during the Blitz, playing their part in the war effort.

Long before the war, not one teaching hospital in London or the provinces would admit black women to train as nurses, and as early as 1933 there had been protests from black organisations regarding this situation. As more and more cases of blatant discrimination were brought to light, and as protests made by the League of Coloured Peoples and other organisations became more voluble, the then home secretary, Mr Anthony Eden, warned that he might act against hotels, restaurants and public houses that refused admission to Indian and African guests on the grounds of their colour, and even spoke of instructing the commissioner of police to refuse to grant licences to such establishments. The Church of England was joined by the Labour Party in condemning discrimination, the party quoted as being 'firmly opposed to it' and the trade unions as having 'cast it aside'. 'Yet,' wrote one contributor to *The Keys*, 'it still persists in the hearts and minds of the people of Britain.' And persist it did.

As the Second World War went on, Dr Moody and his colleagues began to feel and express a growing concern for the welfare of the increasing numbers of 'half-caste' children being born in Britain, their fathers often said to be members of the United States armed forces stationed in Britain. They advertised for a Christian person preferably of colonial origin and black, to carry out a survey of the children and their needs.

The survey was carried out by a Dr Malcolm Joseph-Mitchell, a Trinidadian who had read history and economics at Oxford University. He and Sylvia McNeill, a Jamaican, found it was difficult to ascertain accurately the numbers involved. One reason given was that many mothers moved away from home to other counties and cities, to escape the disgrace and prejudice they encountered. It was found that some mothers were unwilling to part with their children and often lived in appalling conditions, in order to obtain acceptance for themselves and the children. They had good reason to fear at least some of the local authorities, like Somerset, which insisted on taking such children away from their mothers. Destitute mothers reported that when they had approached children's homes, to get their children taken into care, the matrons refused them admission. A solution proposed and favoured by the local authorities, was the use of foster parents, who would give the children a home in return for payment. The Family Welfare Association and Dr Joseph-Mitchell were able to contact some of the children's fathers in America and a few children were actually sent there to be adopted. But there were many more who were unwanted or abandoned.

Various organisations tried opening homes especially for 'half-caste' children. This, of course, meant segregation. There was not much success, although one home in Birkenhead, 'The Rainbow Home', did function for a while; and Dr Joseph-Mitchell himself bought a house in Purley for such children and staffed it with two women who were sympathetic to their needs. Unfortunately, however, it could not function without funding and eventually was closed.

The survey concluded that, although many of the children often lived in disgraceful conditions, they were no more socially disadvantaged than white children in the same area; that the children appeared to have no problems in school and mixed freely; but that when they left school they tended to find their own employment because employment exchanges were rarely helpful.

For a few months after our success with the Newspaper Library and *The Keys*, we seemed to have reached stalemate. We wrote to Lord Wilson of Rievaulx, formerly Sir Harold Wilson, because he featured in a photograph of our father taken by the *Birmingham Mercury*; but he could not recall the occasion. Roy Hattersley, to whom we also wrote, could not help either. Lord Pitt's letter, in which he could remember very little about Ernest, reminded us of the advanced age of some of the people we most needed to meet and talk to: their memories were failing and perhaps we were expecting too much.

Then, just as we were slowing down, a little discouraged, we were given another name and address to visit. Mrs

Rodriguez was Trinidadian, the mother of an acquaintance, and had come to Britain many years previously and was now retired. As we arrived at her house she was looking out for us, eager to talk about Trinidad. She gave us a history lesson and painted a picture of what life may have been like for Ernest as a young man.

Class and caste were the priorities where marriage was concerned: darker-skinned men regarded a marriage or relationship with a lighter-skinned woman as a way to move up in society. Mixed relationships aroused passionate reactions. If a negro boy and an Indian girl, for instance, dared to become involved, the whole community was against it: strong emotions often led to fighting, rioting and even murder between the opposing families.

We recalled that Lynda's aunts, our father's sisters, distanced themselves from her because she married a man much darker than her, who was also of Indian descent. The old men that we spoke to in Trinidad regarded our father's marriage in England as an achievement, and recalled his preference for women who were lighter-skinned than himself.

The war had a major impact on daily life. In Britain our mother had queued for basic foods using her ration books, and in Trinidad mothers had to do likewise. The allowance for rice was a pound per person per week. Mrs Rodriguez recalled that as a child, when she and other young members of the family pounded rice to remove the husks, they often wasted it, and her grandfather warned her that one day they would want for basic food like rice. His words came back to her during the war years when rice, like meat, was rationed. We had never been told of the effects of the war on the Caribbean in our history lessons at school, our thoughts confined only to Europe and the effects of the war on Britain.

The visit to Mrs Rodriguez was good for all three of us. She told us that we had helped to bring her history alive again, and she had brought Trinidad's history alive for us for the first time, evoking even the Pitti Valley near Mareval where Ernest and other young men had strolled many years before.

We began to plan visits to other cities in Britain, our commitment renewed. We wanted to go to Manchester in particular, but also to Birmingham, where our parents had lived. We were in luck: a friend in Manchester offered to introduce us to people she thought could be helpful. This would be our first port of call.

9
Manchester

We arrived in Manchester on a Tuesday evening in July
1989. It was our first visit to the city and we did not know
what to expect. Our friend SuAndi, a performance poet,
drove us through the city pointing out the many historical
landmarks and buildings which are long-established evidence of the presence and hard work of the black citizens,
including herself. She is a woman of mixed race like
ourselves, and knew and understood the longing that had
brought us to her home town. She took us first to meet *her*
father, a Nigerian ex-serviceman who had lived in Britain
for 72 years. We later met another ex-serviceman – an
ex-seaman – Mr Trotter, also over 80 years of age, who
explained how he had arrived in Britain by accident. When
he was 16 years old, in 1924, he and a friend had boarded a
ship in St Lucia just to see what it was like inside. As they
were exploring the ship, it left the island. The young men
were found on board and taken before the captain who
told them the ship could not take them back, but could
employ them: the jobs of galley boy and deck boy were
created specially for them. It was the start of a life at sea.

Although he had come to Britain in completely different
circumstances, Mr Trotter told us a lot about the environment in which Ernest had lived. Mr Trotter had married
but had to go back to sea, knowing his wife would have a
struggle to keep herself and their children. He knew,
however, that the community would not see them suffer.
He described the small black communities in the cities as

'like the islands only colder'. The people were so friendly that no one ever needed to go hungry, he said, everyone looked after each other. He recalled that there seemed to be a special relationship between the black men and the Jewish women in the cities; it was always the Jewish businessmen who gave employment to the black men when no one else would, and when they needed a home, and had to be vouched for as being hardworking and reliable, it was usually their Jewish employers who provided the reference. They often worked alongside the young Jewish girls, some of whom would later become their wives. We thought of Ernest and Elsie.

Such close-knit communities were easy targets for racist attacks. Manchester, Cardiff and Liverpool all experienced riots in 1919. Many black ex-seamen were left unemployed as shipowners devised ways to employ only white British men; although, of course, the black men were all from British territories, and some were even second generation British, coming from families where the father had served the country either as a serviceman or seaman during the First World War. They and their families, already suffering hardship, were subjected to assaults by members of the white community and then arrested for defending themselves.

Most black people in Manchester still live in Moss Side. Many of the black senior citizens we met there told us that they had intended originally to stay only for four or five years. Twenty or thirty years later they sat in the office of their social club explaining to us why they had stayed.

Some had come to Manchester when the government had appealed for workers to come to Britain from the Commonwealth, to help Britain's industry during the postwar boom. Some had come on the advice of other ex-servicemen who had told them that there were opportunities for workers in Britain. And of course there were the ex-servicemen themselves who had seen at firsthand the good as well as the bad in life in Britain during the Second

World War.

The ex-servicemen recalled that the only friends they had in Britain were the women, or the Canadian and New Zealand servicemen. Few British citizens wanted to know them, even though they were fighting for the country and suffered as prisoners of war just as their British counterparts did.

The black population of Manchester consisted of both West Indians and Africans, many of whom were seamen, married to white women, with homes and families established.

On arrival in Britain they usually shared accommodation in rooms let by fellow countrymen or by the wives of black men who had settled in the large cities. Our own mother let rooms to the immigrants our father brought to the house. Once the men had found some space of their own they would purchase a few goods and start saving to send for their wives. Others became involved with local women, married and began families.

Manchester proved to be a valuable source of information for us. We met people who had been part of the black community before the Second World War; and also people like Beverley Lewis, who had been born before the war, to a Nigerian father and a white British mother, and had grown up in Manchester's Moss Side. She was the eldest of three children and learned at an early age to fight and protect her brother and sister from racist remarks and bullying. One of her relatives was married to a black woman and, though she loved her own mother, Beverley felt deeply drawn to this woman whose skin colour and hair were similar to her own. Today Beverley is constantly researching her history and that of the local black community, working to save it for the next generation, to pass it on. With the help of a few others, she has done a lot of work on the fifth Pan African Conference that our father attended, and when we showed her and the others our photograph, they wanted a copy; although they had copies of the press reports, official congress bulletins and some photographs of the main speakers and delegates, they did not have one of the delegates from the Caribbean.

We were told of the concept of 'skin bourgeoisie', which was then in evidence among black people in Britain and surfaced in rivalries at the conference, an echo of the prejudice based on skin tone and inherited from colonialism which we were told had existed in Trinidad. There also existed an educational élitism among black people living in Britain. The small group of intellectuals did not mix with the working men; while the seamen, who were predominantly Africans, on the whole kept themselves apart from other groups. Such divisions were based on class lines rather than those of nationality or island of origin. Black men interacted freely only in the clubs, also often the only places where they felt welcome and could socialise without the threat of hostility.

In her search for information about the Pan African Congress, Beverley had campaigned successfully for the installation of a commemorative plaque on the old town hall building, bearing the names of the main speakers to the conference, including that of Amy Garvey, one of several women who had attended and contributed to the conference, we learned. It would have been wonderful if we could have seen our father's name on that plaque.

We were full of questions for the people we met in Manchester. We were particularly eager to know what Ernest's political background in Trinidad would have been like. As we sat with the older members of the West Indian sports and social club, others passing by stuck their heads around the door and found excuses to come in, find a space and join in the conversation. Everyone was willing to help us and they all had something to offer.

Trini, a club member who had come to Britain 30 years ago, sat upright, cap resting on his knees and spoke in a soft voice. He was five years old when the South Trinidad oilfields uprising occurred in the mid-thirties, and he used to play rather than go to school with his brothers and sisters, so he knew what was happening in the surrounding districts. He began to recall events for us, explaining the background to the uprising.

Indian contract workers and the black descendants of slaves worked as labourers in the docks, oilfields and on the sugar estates. Employers, particularly in the sugar industry, neglected their employees. The men worked in very poor conditions and their families lived in deplorable housing. Wages were extremely low and the management was indifferent to the demands of the workers.

Uriah Butler was one of the leaders of the oilfield workers. Born in Grenada, he had emigrated to Trinidad in 1921, where he worked in the oilfields until he was injured on the job. A religious man, he was also a natural rebel, and fought to ease the poverty of the workers and change their working conditions, encouraging them to demand better safety standards and higher wages by striking for these rights. He was considered to be a threat by both employers and government.

Trini told us that Butler used to attract large crowds to his meetings, who were easily whipped up into an emotional state. It was at one of these meetings that Charlie King, a member of the police force, came to arrest Butler for inciting a riot. Butler had anticipated such a move and used a pre-arranged signal, asking the gathered crowd, 'My people, must I go?' The crowd began to cause a disturbance and he was able to slip away. A woman threw coal oil over Charlie King which burned him to death. Butler hid for some time and when he re-emerged told politicians, 'If you tax my people and take the bread out of their mouths, I will march them across the country again.'

Shortly before Trini came to Manchester, he recalled the time when Princess Elizabeth, now the queen, visited Trinidad. As she processed through one of the districts a Carib woman, who was 113 years of age, walked up and gave her back a medal that had been sent to the woman after King George VI had heard that she was the oldest living resident of the Caribbean. As she handed back the award she told Princess Elizabeth that when she was two years old she and her family had had to hide from British soldiers who were shooting the Caribs – her family and relatives among them – because they refused to be subjected to work for them.

Back in London, at the suggestion of Beverley Lewis, we lost no time in contacting Ernest Marke, and he invited us to come over one Sunday morning. Mr Marke, aged 86, has lived in Britain for over 72 years, since he left Sierra Leone. Between 1917 and 1921 he was a seaman, and he had lived in Liverpool and in Manchester where he met Alma, his first wife, who was also of mixed race. (Her mother had married a black man with the surname Douglas, a word derived from 'Dougla', the Gaelic word for black, used in Trinidad to denote people of mixed African and Indian descent.)

Alma's family experienced a great deal of prejudice at the turn of the century. They were burned out of their home, chased and verbally abused. This happened to many mixed couples before and after the war, and things our mother had said make us think that she experienced this type of abuse too.

After the race riots in Liverpool in 1919 Mr Marke left Britain and travelled to South America and to the United States. On his return he settled in London, became a member of the Coloured Workers' Association, and was also a delegate at the Pan African Congress. As soon as he saw the photograph of our father, he remembered him, and confirmed that Ernest often spent Sunday mornings speaking at Hyde Park Corner, just as C L R James had told us.

More links with Ernest then came out. Mr Marke and our father were both 'kai' showmen, men who sold herbal medicines to the public in market places and fairgrounds, yet another means of earning a living in extremely difficult circumstances when employment – other than as a seaman – was very hard for black men to obtain. One recourse was to set up in business, and Mr Marke did just that, opening a club in Soho in London, in a building in New Compton Street; to our amazement, it turned out to be the same one from which our father had run his business.

Resolve strengthened by our encounters and the information we had elicited from them, we turned our attention to our old home town, Birmingham.

10
Birmingham

Soon after the Manchester visit, we realised that we should
have put an appeal in the Birmingham newspapers for
people to come forward who might have memories of our
father. We enlisted the help of our younger sister who
lived in Birmingham and she sent copies of our request to
the local papers. Two papers published our appeal: *The
Daily News* and *Focus*. We appealed in particular for news of
a couple who had lodged in our home during the war, and
of the family who had lived next door at No. 68.

A few days later we received two letters, followed by a
third several days later. The first was from the widow of a
Trinidadian who had been taught by our father in Trinidad. He had come to Britain and enlisted as an airman
during the war only to find Ernest, his former teacher, in
Britain too. Mrs Chase, his wife, wrote of the first time that
she had met our parents and of her memories of that time.
Her husband, who had died in 1973, had attended our
father's funeral along with a Dr Pilgrim – a fellow Trinidadian. After Ernest's death and our mother's remarriage,
Mrs Chase lost touch with the family. We were excited that
someone who had really known him had replied; and we
realised that it must have been this Mr Chase who had
written to Lynda with news of our father's death.

Mrs Chase confirmed an aspect of Ernest's character that
we had already suspected, his secretiveness: she and her
husband eventually made their home in Birmingham, and
our father used a room in the same house as an office, but

SPEAKING OUT

A voyage round my father

> I AM currently researching a book, which is due to be published next year.
>
> The book is predominantly about my late father, Ernest Mckenzie-Mavinga, who lived in Birmingham from the early 1930s until his death in 1949.
>
> He came originally from Trinidad, where he was a teacher. After his marriage to my mother, Elsie Hart, they lived in Holly Road, Handsworth and then in Stratford Road, Sparkbrook, where I was born.
>
> I feel sure that there are people still living in Birmingham who remember

Thelma Perkins thinks about her father and asks FOCUS readers to help with a book.

this tall black man, who was known for his political views.

During November 1947, he organised a meeting which was covered by the *Mercury* and attended by Harold Wilson.

I am asking people who remember my parents to contact me, especially Ann Gubbins or her mother, who lived next

door to us in Sparkbrook and who will remember our home collapsing about us during January 1955.

I would also like to hear from Moira Berrington and her husband, who lodged with our mother prior to that incident.

I have managed to uncover a great deal about my father's life before he came to England.

Now I would like to fill in the blank spaces of before and during the war years in Birmingham and London. I would be extremely grateful for any help that your readers could give me.

WHAT DO YOU THINK? DROP US A LINE AND WE'LL TRY TO PUBLISH AS MANY OF YOUR SUGGESTIONS AS POSSIBLE!

he would never tell anyone what sort of business he carried on there.

The writer of the second letter, Mr Onslow, wrote of his amazement at seeing a letter in the paper that took him back to his youth 40 years ago. He did not think that he could help us with specific memories of our father, but he was actually very helpful. He and his wife had both grown up in the Small Heath area of Birmingham and could remember the tall 'coloured' gentleman accompanied by a petite white woman. He wrote that later, his elderly father had often spoken of the same person when talking about his memories of the district, and they had often wondered what had happened to Ernest. Mr Onslow had been disabled, using an invalid tricycle to propel himself through the streets, and felt sure that Ernest would have noticed him; perhaps he even felt an affinity for him, as both were in a way disadvantaged.

The most puzzling thing was the use of his office: what

did he do there? And what else did he do? Did he, like the black men today, play cards and dominoes when he met with his contemporaries? Did they bang the dominoes down on the table and shout with enthusiasm as they won the game? Or did they just discuss politics and the oppression of racism which they encountered in their daily lives?

Then the third letter arrived from Kath Murray, a woman who had lived in Henley Street, just around the corner from our old house. After being bombed out the family had moved into 64 Stratford Road, next door to us. Her father used to have a drink in the public house, *The Shakespeare*, with our father, and he had memories of the 'coloured' man who often talked politics, for whom he had great respect and who he regarded as a sort of prophet. Later, we met Kath Murray and she suggested that her mother had been Tod's godmother; they had been staunch Roman Catholics, originating from Ireland, and our father had been a Roman Catholic.

Kath Murray had been a young girl during the war and we were anxious to hear more of her impressions of her first encounters with a black person. We also wondered if she would be able to tell us anything about our mother – her mother and ours must have talked about their lives, their problems and dreams.

A visit to Birmingham and to the writers of these letters would be our next journey. We felt that we were at last getting closer to home, closer to finding out about both our parents socially and emotionally. Perhaps there would be further letters? For the moment we were content that there had been a response; and our only regret was that we had not pursued this aspect of the research earlier.

There is an old Caribbean saying: 'What goes around comes around.' We felt that we had come full circle since that time in 1955 when we had last been in Birmingham together. As our taxi travelled through the city towards the suburbs, we identified landmarks, but most of all were constantly aware that this was only the third time that we had been in our home town together.

We reminisced as we journeyed to meet Mrs Chase. She had known us when we were little children, and had known our parents all those years ago before we had been put into care. We knew she would be able to give us a deeper insight into our family life, into the personal side of Ernest's relationship with our mother, information that until now we had neglected in our search, our focus having been on Ernest, the political and professional man.

We did not know where to start with Mrs Chase, so we began by listening to her tell us about her own life as a white woman married to a Trinidadian who had come to Britain and joined the airforce during the war. She had been engaged, her marriage due to take place within a fortnight, when her sister had asked her to come to a dance. Her sister had said that there would be some 'coloured' airmen there and that she was going out with one of them on a date. Mrs Chase went to the dance and, as she stood waiting for her sister and watching the other dancers arrive, a group of black airmen walked in. She was immediately attracted to one very tall, good-looking young man – 'When I saw him my heart turned over.' He asked her to dance and she knew from that night that she would marry him. She broke off her engagement and some time later married the airman, only discovering afterwards that he was the man her sister was supposed to have been meeting!

She was extremely happy in her marriage and thought on the whole that our parents had been. When she did not see us around, after we had been sent away to the home, she assumed that we had either been evacuated or sent to boarding school. But she did tell us that when she first visited our parents at Stratford Road, our mother had told her, 'You shouldn't marry a coloured man – you won't be happy. Don't tell people that your husband is coloured and if you have any children hide them away. When the welfare

come, don't let them known that your children are
coloured.'

This puzzled us: our mother was telling a friend not to
do as she had done, in marrying our father and bringing us
into the world. There is corroboration of Elsie's feelings in
one of Ernest's letters to the director of the home, however: 'I believe that pressure of the prejudice by her family
and friends caused her not to want the children and not
really her state of health, as she complained about.' We can
only suppose that our mother was not as happy with Ernest
as Mrs Chase originally had assumed.

Mrs Chase had had more contact with Ernest than with
our mother. Her husband had taken her to meet our
parents soon after the marriage and Mrs Chase had spent a
weekend in our home. Her husband was away in the air
force and she often turned to Ernest for advice, when she
had difficulties with her landlord, or other problems. The
house that she lived in was multi-tenanted, with many
rooms, all with shared kitchen and bathroom facilities.
Ernest also rented a small room there and used it as an
office. She used to hear the sound of his typewriter as he
worked long hours in the room.

She conjured up an image for us of a busy man who
liked children and who would always find the time to talk
with her and her own young daughters. At one point her
husband brought home an abandoned baby of mixed race
and she cared for the child along with her own children for
some time. Ernest advised her in this case to put the child
into a home; and we recognised wryly how secretive a
person he was, that he had not told Mrs Chase where his
own children were.

Towards the end of his life Ernest was ill. Mrs Chase told
us about Dr Pilgrim, Ernest's doctor, and his warning to
Ernest only three weeks before he died. Our father was
suffering from gout, as well as being a diabetic, and Dr
Pilgrim told him that he had to change his drinking habits
or he would not live much longer. He died three weeks

later, and Mrs Chase's husband and the doctor attended his funeral with our mother, and witnessed the cremation of his body. Mrs Chase had not gone herself but was able to convey, even after all those years, her husband's feelings as we sat and listened.

It was a relief for Isha in particular to hear that people were physically close to Ernest at the end of his life. It took her a step beyond the day she visited the place where his ashes were scattered. Listening to Mrs Chase helped to take away the sad feeling that nobody cared, nobody was there and that no one seemed to know where his remains were laid to rest. It made Isha feel closer to Ernest, and we both left the house feeling satisfied. We had made a journey and, through another person's memories, had reached the end of Ernest's life.

We travelled next to Erdington to meet the Onslows. They had told us all they knew in their letter and in a subsequent telephone call, but they still wanted to meet us and we were hungry for their memories.

Our first question was whether they could recall what they had each felt the first time they had seen our father, the first black man that they had ever seen in their lives. (They did not know each other then, even though they lived in the same district.) Mrs Onslow could remember precisely. She was probably about eight years old and had been playing outside in the front garden of her Small Heath home. It was a Sunday and she could only play outside if she were quiet. Our father walked past their garden and she ran indoors to ask her father, who was a scientist, about him. He sat her down and gave her a scientist's explanation about the existence of black people.

Her husband had been disabled from early childhood. On Sunday afternoons until he was able to manipulate his invalid tricycle himself and go out on his own, his father often used to push him along the Coventry Road and around the Small Heath area, which was always quiet at that time of the day. It was during these walks that they often saw Ernest walking with his arm around a small white lady, whom they presumed was his wife.

When we showed them a photograph they recognised him immediately. They told us that he looked 'noble', was very tall and always wore dark three-piece suits.

Mr Onslow's recollections of the Second World War brought our parents' Birmingham alive. Most working people had jobs in the factories of Dunlop, Lucas, BSA, Rover and Cadbury. During the war, most factories converted to producing supplies and munitions in particular for Britain's war effort, which made them prime targets for German bombing raids. The workforce then consisted mainly of women and girls, as men aged between 18 and 65 who were exempt from military service were generally members of the Home Guard.

The real bombardment of Birmingham began during 1940, a year in which the winter was particularly severe. On one night in 1941, according to the BBC, over 100 factories were hit by bombs and more than 300 fires raged across the city; between 1940 and 1943 there were 77 air raids.

The city's black community was very small then, and as well as men from the Caribbean and Africa, there were about 100 Asians, mostly students studying medicine or law. Black medical professionals had until then been unable to practise in hospitals but they were soon accepted as they worked to help rescue the victims of the air raids. Sparkbrook and Small Heath were subjected to heavy bombing raids, with some factories receiving direct hits. Many homes were rendered uninhabitable by bomb damage.

Once the United States had become involved in the Second World War, then local people began to see more 'coloured' men. On Saturday evenings, lorries full of American servicemen would be driven down Coventry Road into Birmingham city centre, where they would dance and relax and for a while forget the trials of war. The servicemen, white and black, were an abundant source of chocolates and nylons for the young women who went out with them, who spent many hours queuing for basic necessities, longing for the luxuries that the US allies could supply.

Sunday afternoons, when there was a short respite from the German bombs, must have seemed so peaceful for everyone. Often the children would be packed off to Sunday school for a couple of hours in the afternoon, and there would be time for harassed and tired mothers and fathers, if they were at home, to sleep. Others would take a peaceful walk around the district or in the local park, just as our father had done with our mother.

Leaving the Onslows' bungalow, we could not stop talking about what they had said, and imagining our parents' lives.

That just left Kath Murray who had actually lived next door to us during the war. After being bombed out, her Irish family was forced to move, and was given accommodation by the man who owned Nos. 62 and 64 Stratford Road. She was about 11 years old when this happened and recalled that a lot of people in the street would not speak to our mother, probably because she was married to a black man. But Kath Murray's own mother suffered discrimination because the family was Irish, and the two women therefore felt a bond, and used to visit each other and chat over cups of tea. Similarly, it was her father who would drink with our father in the local public house that stood on the corner of Henley Street.

Kath could recall her father saying that the conversation was mainly political, but that Ernest always had time for people, whatever their politics. People in the community got to know him. He would join in with the other men after an air raid and help rescue people. The BSA factory, which manufactured ammunition during the war, suffered a direct hit on 7 April 1941 and the BBC reported that 53 workers were killed. All the men in the area were soon on the scene and our fathers worked alongside each other trying to clear the debris in search of survivors, racial barriers crumbling temporarily.

Many young children were frightened of black people, because parents often threatened them with 'The Bogeyman', who was assumed to be black. Kath Murray had firsthand experience of contact with a black man and was not frightened of him. He often talked to her and always gave her pennies for sweets. Her memory is of a 'coloured' man at least six foot four inches tall, with a trilby hat which he always doffed to ladies and a scarf around his neck.

She recalled an occasion when she had taken her younger sister out to buy sweets. Clutching her sister with one hand and their ration book with the other as she went down the road, they met Ernest.

'Hallo, little girls,' he said, bending down to them.

'Hallo, black face,' replied her sister, completely unabashed.

Our father seemed unoffended and gave them a few pennies to supplement the ones that they already had.

We felt, after all these exchanges, that we had returned to our beginnings and that the people we had met had helped bring our father alive for us.

11
Ernest's Story

Throughout our search we have been asking ourselves, 'Who was Ernest? Who was our father?' We have written countless letters, travelled many miles and spoken to many, many people, turning stone after stone.

We think that he was born in 1898 into a relatively well-off family. For a young man with a dark skin in Trinidad at that time, he was fortunate to get a good education. In about 1914 he became a prefect teacher, went on to the government teacher training college and then, by about 1918, to his first teaching post in Tobago. By now he had married and his only surviving child, a daughter Lynda, was born in 1922 back in Trinidad, where he got a job teaching at Nelson Street Primary School and, by the late 1920s had become its vice principal. But he was beginning to get itchy feet, and in 1927, when he was 29 years old, he set sail for London.

He grew up in a time when black professionals were beginning to agitate for a place in the hierarchy that ruled Trinidad. People were hungry for change. They wanted social acceptance, political change and better working conditions. There was discrimination in all areas of employment. The tone of a person's skin played a major part in determining whether they were employed or not and in what capacity. The island's economy was growing, but the workers were not enjoying the benefits. Prices continued to rise, particularly those of staple goods, while the workers' wages continued to be heavily taxed.

One of the new political leaders who emerged after the First World War was Arthur Andrew Cipriani. He was of mixed race and had risen to the rank of captain while serving with the West Indies regiment in Europe during the First World War, and returned to the Caribbean feeling very bitter about the discrimination he and others like him had encountered.

War veterans such as these became supporters of Cipriani, and looked towards him and other new black leaders like Marcus Garvey and W E B DuBois. Ernest knew some of the black leaders who were agitating for change, and admired their political fervour and goals: the respect that he felt for them personally was reflected in his choice of names for our brothers, which were those of two famous black leaders, Andrew Arthur Cipriani and 'Teddy' Albert Marryshow. Marryshow, a Grenadian, had lived in Britain for many years, becoming a prominent representative of Britain's black communities, who voiced his opinions on the effects of colonialism in the Caribbean, particularly in Grenada where, in some instances, people worked for one halfpenny per day.

Ernest and other of his contemporaries travelled to Britain after the First World War in order to study, some chose medicine, others literature and others politics. They dispersed throughout Britain from London to Edinburgh, joining a small group of Africans and Indians who were already studying there, some of whom later became noted leaders of newly independent countries.

Ernest had planned to study, and journalism was his first choice. But when he was unable to pursue this course he opted to study draughtsmanship at Leicester, a project that fell through, he believed, because of the colour bar.

In Britain his interest in politics continued; he met and made friends from Trinidad and they discussed international politics and the future for black countries. He continued to play a part in the anti-racist movement in

Britain until his death.

His first wife, who had remained in Trinidad, died and he met and married our mother. Arranging conferences and discussing politics could not pay for a home, a wife and a growing family. He had to find a means of support: he was an entrepreneur, a film extra, a 'kai' showman and then he set up the Caribbean Bureau in New Compton Street.

Throughout this period, he wrote. Short stories, poems and plays. According to those who knew him, like all aspiring authors he submitted his work to potential publishers – the BBC, Reader's Digest and others, hoping for recognition and acceptance. We have not been able to find out whether he was ever successful in this; all his manuscripts were stored in the attic of the house on Stratford Road and disappeared under rubble when the house collapsed.

Political meetings and discussions continued to be important to him, but his main problem was to safeguard his children and their upbringing. He eventually took them to the children's home in Chislehurst, after his plan to take them to Trinidad had failed, partly, according to his own account, because of his wife's opposition. He began to travel regularly around the country and back and forth to Trinidad.

He had told his family in Trinidad that he planned to go to Africa. Some of his contemporaries who had completed their medical studies were practising on the Gold Coast (later Ghana) and in Sierra Leone, something that was common among Caribbean doctors early in their careers. We would like to believe that he did go to Africa and fulfil his ambition. Certainly it was during this time that he adopted the name Mavinga. (We have no idea where he got the name from; the only Mavinga in the *Times Atlas* index is a town in southern Angola and we do not know if there is any connection.) There is also the six-year gap (1942–8) between our births, which suggests that he may have been away from our mother, perhaps on a long journey, for at least part of that time. But there is nothing to prove he did go. His first passport is missing; the second passport was issued during 1942, and indicates only travel to Trinidad. We have never seen or found artefacts or any other evidence that would confirm a visit to Africa.

At the end of the Second World War, our father appears to have stayed for most of the time in Birmingham, although he maintained his office in London. He visited his children in Chislehurst regularly and took them home for holidays. He was photographed at the Pan African Conference to which he was a Caribbean delegate. He met and mingled with popular public figures, Joe Louis the boxer, among them. And he continued to speak publicly about the causes dear to his heart.

Ernest was often away from home, and we now know that he spent time in most of Britain's major cities, including London, Bristol and Liverpool, where he always found hospitality and, importantly, a refuge from the isolation which Ernest would have felt in a city like Birmingham with no established black community. As he was a traveller who enjoyed meeting people, a man who was obviously widely known, we have wondered whether he had relationships with other women; although we have not found anyone else linked with him in this country. We have frequently met and made friends with other people whose surname is McKenzie and have pondered the possibility of a family connection, particularly with one or two who have borne a remarkably close resemblance to ourselves. But so far, other than Lynda, we have not traced any other brothers and sisters, nor other family members.

Early in 1990 our search seemed to be coming to an end, although we knew that there was still more to discover about Ernest. Peter Fryer had suggested in his letter to us that we contact Len Garrison, who has been responsible for setting up the Black Archives Museum in London. He showed the same enthusiasm as most people had in response to our search, which he thought would produce useful material for the Black Archives Museum. From a list of contacts with which he supplied us, the most successful meeting was with 'Uncle' Malcolm.

To our amazement he turned out to be Dr Malcolm Joseph-Mitchell, who had carried out the research about children of mixed race for *The Keys*. He had also known Ernest. Malcolm still teaches economics, which he studied at Oxford University, where he was a member of the 'varsity' athletics team. He was also captain of the West Indian team that competed in the Empire games in Australia in 1939.

Malcolm invited us to come up and have tea with him. He was keen to see whether we looked like Ernest, and we were eager to hear his memories of our father.

It was Malcolm who told us about the failed restaurant venture in Liverpool and recalled in detail for us Ernest's political commitment to Caribbean nationalism and to the struggle of black people everywhere, and many other vivid impressions.

Malcolm had not known Ernest in Trinidad but had known his sister and the house on the corner of a street in St Joseph where Ernest's family lived.

Later, when Malcolm was living in Britain, and had just competed in the track events of an athletics meeting held at Stamford Hill, Ernest had suddenly appeared in the changing room, and greeted Malcolm by saying, 'Don't tell me that you don't know me. Your father gave me more lickings than he ever gave you.' Ernest went on to tell him that, as a schoolboy attending Richmond Street School in Port of Spain, he had been recognised as a pupil with potential, and had been sent to Malcolm's father who was the principal of Tranquillity School, another local institution, for private tuition. Malcolm's father had evidently used physical means to instil knowledge in his pupil.

At that point Malcolm realised who Ernest was and

remembered throwing stones at the mango tree that stood in the front garden of his home. From then on, Malcolm became Ernest's protégé. Mac, as he called Ernest, had been as proud of Malcolm's achievements and his interest in sport as if he had been Ernest's brother or son, and Malcolm was always assured of one immaculately dressed spectator cheering for him when he competed in athletics events.

Malcolm was impressed by Ernest's striking personality. Ernest liked to talk and joke, but never talked much about his personal life and, in Malcolm's view, if Ernest *had* written his autobiography he probably did not complete it: he was full of ideas, a 'dabbler' who often started things he did not finish – no doubt he was too busy hustling for a living, trading in any commodity he could buy at the docks in Liverpool and sell at his office in New Compton Street.

Ernest was always a perfect gentleman, immaculately dressed, with a walking stick. He used to tell Malcolm, 'You should always carry yourself properly even if you are down.' Malcolm described him as 'bespoke and charismatic'. People were attracted to him: often they thought he was wealthy and tried to sponge off him, but he dealt with their demands by always seeming too busy to stop and chat for long.

Ernest introduced Malcolm to many important people. They visited Paul Robeson when he stayed in London at the home in St John's Square of Leslie 'Hutch' Hutchinson, a singer and pianist; and met C L R James, Marcus Garvey, Aneurin Bevan, Lord Soper, Barbara Castle (then Barbara Betts) and Fenner Brockway.

They would often meet at a venue in Leicester Square, have coffee in the Lyons Corner House at Charing Cross, or walk on a Sunday morning to Hyde Park Corner to listen to the speakers (although Malcolm himself never heard Ernest speak there) and whenever Malcolm was in London he would eat at a club-cum-restaurant that Ernest ran, with another black man, in Shaftesbury Avenue.

At one time, Malcolm remembers, Ernest disappeared and it was rumoured that he had died.

'Ernest used to say to me, "When someone can't be found, ask him how much he owes you." But he didn't owe me anything . . . I can still see that scamp right in front of me,' Malcolm told us.

He was surprised to learn of Ernest's wife and children in Birmingham.

'Ah,' he said, 'so that's what he meant when he used to say, "Keep your hands in your pockets, never let your left thumb know what your right thumb's doing".'

When Ernest's new daughter, Jane, was born in 1948 he wrote to the children's home with the news. But he gave no indication that he planned to send her there too; perhaps he wanted to keep her at home. We do know though that shortly after Jane's birth, his health began to deteriorate. Five months later he was dead.

12
And What Are We?

We grew up as 'white-thinking' children of mixed race, with the same missionary attitudes to black people that most white people had. The hymns we sang in Sunday school and the illustrations in our story and school books told of uneducated savages with unkempt hair, grass skirts or, worse, no clothes at all, who carried spears, beat drums and uttered unintelligible noises. They did not believe in Jesus.

We did not associate ourselves with these images. We did not think beyond our immediate surroundings. Our world was far removed from that of our 'Little brown brothers and sisters', whom we were taught about in the home and who were, like us, 'children of Christ, spiritual brothers and sisters': any more tangible, realistic comparisons between ourselves and the children of heathens went unimagined. We were totally ignorant of black culture, language and food, although these should have been important aspects of our upbringing. In the home children were not seen as individuals; we were an undifferentiated group. No matter that *we* had brown skin and black curly hair that required special treatment. The aunties just sidestepped the issue. And nowhere was this more in evidence than in the attitude to hair. Our white sisters all had long hair braided in two long plaits, long because Solomon had decreed that a woman's hair was her crowning glory; but our hair was cropped short, because it was easier to manage.

Tod

I remember for years my ambition was to have my hair long enough to wear in a pony tail. I didn't understand that I lacked one because I was a little black girl with Afro hair that was difficult to manage. Most of the girls I was growing up with had hair long enough to sit on. My hair was probably cut whenever I went home to visit our mother. One of mother's brothers had a fish and chip shop, and he acted as my barber. I loved going to visit him. After he had cropped my hair, I used to stuff myself with potato chips fried in his shop.

Isha

I also longed to have a pony tail, to have long hair. As I grew older, I used to copy hairstyles from women's magazines, which all depicted white female teenagers rolling up their hair. My attempts to do this with my Afro hair usually failed, until I was able to have my hair straightened with setting gels.

We did not know that the colour of our skin was inherited from our black father. Isha remembers being frightened of people darker than her and feels she would not have had those negative feelings if she had known our father.

For Tod it was different, as she at least remembers him. But, in any case, we were not conscious of our parents' colour. We did not know them very well, but the important thing was that they were our parents.

As we grew older, we became aware that we were different from both the white children we grew up with, and the black people who were beginning to settle in Britain. As teenagers we got verbal abuse from white people; but we were often asked if we thought ourselves too good for black people, when we ignored the black men who called out to us in the street, and black girls at school were quick to abuse anyone with a lighter skin. We were not white, but to some, our lighter skin meant that we were not black either.

Decades later, we are still trying to define ourselves. We are British because we were born in Britain and our mother was British; our father was Trinidadian and we can claim his nationality. We have the genes, the characteristics and the colouring of both our white mother and our black father. The Hart and McKenzie-Mavinga lines are both very strong. All our brothers and sisters have inherited aspects of our mother's and our father's physical appearances and we can see them in our own children, in our mother's relatives – on the rare occasions we meet them – and now, in Lynda and her family.

The label 'mixed race', a sociologist's definition, automatically implies problems, perhaps because it is a label; for at least 45 years, those of us affected by labelling have been trying to change attitudes that, unfortunately, still persist, along with the labels. For example, a letter to *The Keys* in December 1945, from a person labelled 'half-caste', argued that children whose fathers hailed from Africa or the West Indies usually acknowledged their mixed parentage but identified with their father's nationality; and the writer asked for more tolerance and understanding from coloured people and less use of the pejorative word 'half-caste'. This is why being labelled 'mixed race' is an issue for us: because society talks about us as if we are abnormal, inevitable misfits.

The more we learn about ourselves as black women, the more we know about who we are, where we come from and where we belong, the more we recognise how wrong society is. What do young black British people have to do to be accepted as British? Do we have to win a gold medal at the Olympics for our nationality to be confirmed?

In America black people are referred to as Afro-American, a title which, while acknowledging the origins of black people, also acknowledges their right to citizenship. But black people in Britain, regardless of their place of birth, are always identified as West Indian, or Afro-Caribbean. Our father, before he died, helped to organise a conference to tackle this issue, and to demand equality for all black children born in Britain.

Our lives began as black babies; we grew up as white teenagers; now we are black adults and, in the process of finding out about Ernest, have become black sisters.

Undoubtedly, one of the reasons for prejudice against children of mixed race is a generalised pessimism about the viability of their parents' relationships. Now we have learned more about our father and his Caribbean culture we wonder why he was attracted to our mother. She was a white Jewish girl from a working-class background. He was a black professional and a member of the Pan African movement with strong political views. Who did he share his anger with when he saw the way black people were being treated at that time? We have learned that he discussed his sense of disillusion with other black men in other cities in Britain and that they gave each other support. But was he supported by our mother when he raised a political issue, or did she not understand?

She obviously had fears about their relationship and its rightness, and about the future of her black children. Why else did she advise another woman to hide the colour of her children from the authorities and to conceal her relationship with her husband?

Ernest himself was successfully hiding his relationship and his children from some of the people who knew him. His reasons for doing so were complex: on the one hand, perhaps a 'skin bourgeoisie' was in operation at that time among intellectual black men in Britain, and perhaps it was that which motivated his need to fit into a white culture, and also motivated his attraction to our mother; on the other hand, there was prejudice against such marriages and 'half-caste' children, and perhaps it was his need to remain within the black community that caused him to deny our existence to some people. We now believe that the reluctance to talk that we encountered during our ten-year search for information about Ernest was the result of our parents' secrecy. The people we met were doubtful about talking to us because they had never known we existed.

We have found it difficult to find any positive aspects in our parents' relationship, although we have met other black and white couples of their generation who met, fell in love and made lasting relationships.

One thing that has continued to puzzle us is our mother's marriage to Jimmy after Ernest's death. We have tried to fathom her decision: why didn't she leave and make a completely new life for herself? Why did she marry another black man? Did she really imagine that her life would be better than before?

Jimmy was as secretive as Ernest about his family background. Our mother knew nothing about his family in the Caribbean, and did not really know his friends in Britain. Tod remembers that occasionally on Saturdays he would go out to the barber's and would stay out all day. It appeared that this was the time that he visited his friends. He was very quiet but would sometimes recall anecdotes about life in Trinidad, and also had a fund of jokes and quotations that he would narrate at an opportune moment.

It seemed that he could relate better to babies and very young children for as Tod grew older and when her brothers returned to live at home he grew more and more introverted, until he hardly communicated with them at all.

He was very conscientious, working at a metal works in a dirty backbreaking job and travelling for long hours to and from the factory. One morning he collapsed with pneumonia as he prepared to leave for work and our mother relived all the anxiety that she had experienced when Ernest became ill and died. Jimmy survived; but shortly afterwards they both suffered the shock of the house collapsing and from then on both Jimmy's and our mother's health deteriorated.

The marriage also did nothing to reduce Elsie's isolation. She still had no close friends. Visitors to the house were few. Her only confidante was her sister Bella, who had shared the first house that Ernest had provided as a home for our mother. Her neighbours on the Stratford Road were there to help in an emergency but she rarely stood and talked with them over the fence. The neighbours' daughter was only ever allowed to play 'through the fence' with our younger sister; never in the same yard.

After they had moved to Ladywood, our mother did form a friendship with her immediate neighbour. They shared cups of tea in our house and the children played together in the yard. However, she never went to visit friends or enjoyed an evening out with Jimmy. It was only very rarely that she attended even the welfare clinic. Most mothers of young children made regular visits to the clinic, where they made friends and compared the way their babies were developing. But our mother stayed at home and sent Thelma to collect the free orange juice and milk that all babies were entitled to once a month.

So although Jimmy provided for and stayed with his family, life for our mother could not really have been much better. She still had to struggle financially and she still suffered racial abuse. When our father died she sent his youngest child into care. She was free to start a new life, to improve the strained relationship with her own family and to earn a living for herself. For nearly 15 years she had suffered some degree of social exclusion as a result of her marriage to our father, which had been barely tolerated, and her family must have felt a measure of relief when she was widowed and able to start an independent life. But instead she married another black man and had three more children whom she had to protect from racial abuse.

Throughout our search we have continually asked ourselves why we children were really placed in care and whether the reasons were valid, or whether our parents wanted us out of the way. Against which parent should we direct our anger? Could a woman really give birth to four children, breastfeed them for months and then let them be taken away without protest and placed with other children in the care of total strangers?

Other women brought up families singlehandedly with very little financial aid. In cities like Manchester, Liverpool and Cardiff, other white women brought up their black children in equally difficult conditions.

If our father loved us and was so proud of us, why did he send us so far away? He had friends who were white; couldn't they have helped our mother through her difficult times? Couldn't our parents have supported each other? Were they to blame?

At the time we were born, there was a myth that helped to fuel postwar racism: people were led to believe that thousands of black babies were being born, the fathers being those who came from the colonies to study and serve in the British and United States armed forces during the Second World War. Attitudes such as these exacerbated the already considerable difficulties being faced by Ernest and Elsie.

Ernest had been able to provide a good home for our mother. Unfortunately, the subtle ways in which men like our father were prevented from pursuing their chosen courses of study and subsequent careers meant that he had to be away from home in order to earn a living and maintain living standards.

Our mother experienced racism from her neighbours and her family (although as prejudiced as the family members were against the marriage, they always treated the children with affection). The week before she died the house was full of her relatives. After her funeral none of them ever visited Jimmy or her children again. She had had to face such hostility alone, at a time when she was undergoing the stress of night-time bombing raids on the city. We know that the pressure caused her ill health, and that these problems, her isolation, anxiety and illness may have been some of the reasons that she wanted to hide the fact of the children's existence and eventually had us put into care. Ernest must have realised this and thought that his children would be better cared for in Trinidad.

There was obviously a struggle between them over our welfare resulting in Elsie preventing Ernest from taking the children out of the country. He then had to search for the home that would give the children the best care that he could find in Britain. Later, he felt it necessary to write to the superintendent of the home telling her of the dispute between him and Elsie, and rebuking her and Mr Davidson as professed Christians, for misrepresenting his motives for placing the children in care. He felt strongly enough about the accusations to take the risk of writing: the home could have responded by sending the children back.

66 Stratford Road
Birmingham
24 July 1945

Mrs Davidson
Superintendent
Barbican Home for Jewish Children
Mt Zion
Chislehurst, Kent

Dear Madam,

A fortnight ago Mrs McKenzie and I called at Mt Zion to see the children. We saw them and have been very pleased with their condition. I have been somewhat disappointed in not meeting you or Mr Davidson, as I desired to make some arrangements for liquidating arrears and beginning to pay for the children according to agreements signed by me. I shall, however, notify you when I will be next calling at the home, and if it be convenient to meet Mr Davidson, I should be pleased to.

Since my return, Mrs McKenzie and I had some talk regarding the future of the children. In the course of one of these talks she accused me of making a false statement about her to you or Mr Davidson, to wit, that I said that she had left me and gone away which caused me to apply to you to take over the children. I refuse to believe that such a statement was made by you maliciously. It certainly must have been a mistake. What I am positive that I stated in my letter to Mr Davidson was that I believe that pressure of the prejudice by her family and friends caused her not to want the children, and not really her state of health, as she complained about. My opinion then and now is based on observation and not merely a question of fantastic thought.

I do not know if in Mrs McKenzie's conversations with you she was truthful enough to tell you that I provided her with a beautiful home, in one of the best residential quarters of Birmingham. On her own persistent request, I had to find her somewhere else, our present address. During the period 1941–2, she complained of too much work with the children, although it was only the house work she had to attend to. Consequently, the children had to be shifted into one or other of the Birmingham Municipal Homes from time to time. Then I finally decided to apply to you. That is the position as it stood. For me then the home became empty and I decided to leave for my homeland to establish there and get them over as soon as I had fully settled down. That would have happened were it not for representations which can only be set down to ignorance that my wife made to the British government. Those representations stood in my way. I had to alter my plans; and for the sake of the children decided to come back and start all over again.

Another point I want to make clear is that it is very rare you find that a negro is just a professed Christian. As a matter of fact, the negro is invariably, a born Christian, so unlike the white man. He is always a practical one. The churches are empty in England. In my country, they are always filled. That, however, is not so much an index of their innate Christianity as their adherence to the elementary principle of true Christianity as laid down by Christ . . . That is: 'Do not do unto others as you would not have done unto you.' The fatherhood of God and the brotherhood of man is our motto; not in theory, but in practice.

Regretting to have had to send you what you may think a homily.

I remain,
Yours faithfully,

E McKenzie-Mavinga

Isha

For most of my life I have wallowed in bitterness towards my lost parents and the family life I have been denied; until Tod showed me the correspondence between our parents and the home. After reading it, I began to understand some of the struggles my parents had to face, which accounted for the struggles I had faced as a child. They explained why my mother felt she had to put me in care. I had not just been dumped because my father had died, as had been my first impression. However, it seems to me now that my mother's family, with whom I have had virtually no contact and of whom I know very little, seems to bear at least some of the responsibility for my parents' struggles and my consequent loss.

Tod

Dear Isha,

When our mother put you into the arms of the woman who ran the home, she had no intention of abandoning you. For years she must have felt guilty and indeed full of pain: the same pain she felt when she gave birth, the same pain you and I felt when our daughters left us before we were ready to let them go.

Just as you spent a lot of time waiting for her to visit you, to have you home for the holidays, she must have planned to visit, to have you home for the holidays. But all her life poverty dogged her, from childhood through to death, clinging to her like a shadow, refusing to be shaken.

Meeting our father, this tall, 'dark', handsome gentleman, must have been like a fairy tale. He probably made her promises of a better life, probably swept her off her feet, entranced her with tales of the Caribbean and his planned travels in the African continent. Did he ever tell her of his dead wife and dear daughter in Trinidad? Did she know that while she was giving birth to their first son, his daughter had already made him a grandfather? She never told me if she did.

I grieve for the woman who did not even confide in her sisters, who felt so alone in her relationship that she locked it all away and, when she died, left us no past and so many unanswered questions. And when our father died taking his past with him what did she do? She married another black man! What was she looking for? She was not trapped then: her children were in care, out of sight. So the wheel kept on turning, struggle and strife, more babies, but not more money. She must have promised herself a thousand times that the next Christmas she would have you home. But it only happened once and even then your fare must have cost her a great deal.

Isn't it strange, little sister, how the years have passed and no one can answer our questions? Who will tell us the truth, and whose truth will it be? The letters from our father to the woman who gave us a home, say that our mother couldn't cope with us because she was unwell. What did that mean? Our aunts, her sisters, say that our father – the perfect gentleman – was often away for long periods, leaving our mother without enough money to care for us. I feel that perhaps she could not cope as a white woman with three black babies in a hostile family; yet, I can remember the uncles, her brothers who took me out, treated me, made a fuss of me, the kisses of grandma, her mother, and the welcoming smiles of the aunts, her sisters.

Ernest, our father, gave her a roof over her head, that's true. But he pursued his political interests, his journalism and his life all around Britain while she struggled at home in Birmingham. We went into the home and for five years until she became pregnant with you there were no children to cope with. I was three months old when our brothers and older sister were collected from the Erdington cottage children's home – dirty, louse-ridden and ill – and taken to Chislehurst to the white aunties who were to parent us.

What did our mother do during those five years before you were conceived? She did visit us regularly, we went home every Boxing Day for at least two weeks and sometimes also after camp in the summer, where we were spoiled, fed and given attention by her, and her brothers and sisters.

The aunties in the home cared for us as best they knew how. One or two who did not like children treated all of us abominably, but they were outnumbered by the staff who genuinely loved all children and tried their best to give us a home and a caring environment in which to grow up.

Can you believe that, although we were separated from you, all four of us received more affection and attention than the others *because* of our colour? (Even our oldest sister, who is white, revealed many years later how jealous she felt of us.) No one had ever seen black babies before: we were better dressed, we were taken out individually and, yes – even you were spoiled by the staff.

As a small child you were loved, but as you grew older so did the world you lived in, and the nature of the home and the staff who ran it changed. Those women who had babied you and cared for you, went off to become the wives of missionaries, or moved on to other situations, and the staff who took over were not the same. Your school had other black children as well as you; I had been alone in all the schools I had attended. Now you were seen as *different* by those who had previously thought of you as *special*. They had someone to compare you with, perhaps they expected you to behave like the 'newcomers' who were regarded as foreigners.

Changes of a lifetime in only six years. Your years from puberty to adulthood were so different from mine. I did not suffer the unhappiness you did. I can also look at your early years from a different perspective. Don't be sad, little sister, now you are grown and have come to terms with your past: feel for our parents who left us the task of building our futures on a legacy of silence and uncertainty.

While we were writing this book we have been taking sides. One of us tended to take our mother's side having had the experience of living at home with her as a teenager and

seeing the kind of life she was living. The other has
defended our father because of her need for the father she
never had and to recover parts of a history that seemed lost
for ever.

These past ten years have been a journey into our own
existence. A journey where we have met and talked to
people who knew Ernest but who did not know that we
existed. Our parents excluded us from their life, their
struggle. We have had to struggle to include ourselves in
their lives.

We have discovered from our school reports that both of
us could have gone to a grammar school. At the age of 11
we both got borderline passes in the eleven-plus exam. We
were both refused entry on interview, but if we had got
those places and then gone on to higher education all those
years ago, we might not have become mature students or
begun to explore our black history. For everything there is
a time, a season; for us it was not when we were 11 years
old. Our time, our season, is now.

We have been a long time growing. It has taken ten years
to gather the information for this book and for our
relationship as sisters to mature.

We can never replace the years when we should have
been a family together. We are alike in that we share
similar experiences as black women: both of us are now
grandmothers, with a responsibility to pass on our heritage
to our own families, making blackness positive in all our
lives. But we do not share the same views on all aspects of
our past.

Discovering who Ernest was has filled a gap in our lives.
It has also contributed to our relationships with the black
men in our lives. In our early years we did not have any
male role models. Our search during these ten years has
given us the opportunity to talk with mature black men,
many of whom are fathers. The intellect, humour, story-
telling, political views, interests and varying capacity for

taking responsibility in these men were traits that we could imagine in our father.

Not all our history has been uncovered. We have not discovered evidence of any relatives on Ernest's side of the family, as we were only able to go back as far as our paternal grandfather. We may not have been able to go back much further anyway: people were scattered by slavery, and the thousands of slaves taken by force to work in the Caribbean left all their history behind on the African continent, forced to discard their given names, which could have given clues to their places of origin, and to reject traditional customs which would have enabled their descendants to retain their heritage. This has delayed black people's search for their African roots.

However, although we have not been successful in tracing Ernest's African roots, we have met black women who are part of our family, a sister, Lynda, and nieces, and forging a link with them has helped to reinforce our relationship as women together. (Our search uncovered the rest of our family but it also meant the loss of one member. Our eldest sister, Sheila, our mother's first child whom Ernest had adopted and who had shared all the same privations as us, chose to withdraw from us during the period that we began to discover our identity as black women. For Tod, it meant the loss of a relationship that had deepened since the death of our mother, while Isha, who had only just begun to know her, felt that she had lost an opportunity.) Lynda mothered other children who had no parents. She told us that if she had known about us she would have taken us in and mothered us too. No other women in our family have sent their children away and it has never occurred to us not to look after our own children.

It is because of our experiences of all the women in our lives that we have been able to nurture and mother our own children and keep them with us. First, our mother breastfed us. Then, in the home, there were short periods when we were very young that we remembered being hugged, sitting on 'mother's' knee; having 'auntie' all to ourself; being taken out by an older girl. These were important experiences that we have reproduced in rearing our own families. Then, when we were adolescents Tod mothered our mother's second family in Birmingham while Isha, still in the home, was yearning for mothering.

We were far away from each other then and now realise that during this period we ourselves were not being mothered. Having come to understand our parents' motives, we are still feeling the pain of not having had that experience for most of our childhood. We have learned to care for our children without the support of an extended family. Now we are beginning to build an extended family with our children, encouraged by knowing Lynda and finding out about family life in Trinidad – an experience our father wanted us to have.

Isha

Tod, I feel that you have changed while we have been writing this book. It seems as though some of the way that I am has rubbed off on you: I see you as being more like me now. What I mean is that you share some of my knowledge and my ideas. I feel that I have become less of you, which means that now I am much less likely to be influenced by your ideas. Because you are older than me and in the past have been more like a mother, I looked at what you were doing and listened to what you were saying, and was influenced in many ways by your actions. I am ten and you are sixteen years old when we are together!

Tod

I have been aware of the changes taking place in you from before we began to work together on this book. They began when you divorced your husband and gradually became more assertive. Somehow it is as if you only began your life when you reached thirty. I can now understand why you feel ten years old when you are with me.

I wasn't aware of the sort of person that you were before then. You were just my sister. And, as you have said, I was really – consciously or unconsciously – mothering you. I know now that until you began to assert yourself as a woman, a mother and a person in your own right I didn't really know you. I have to admit that I was surprised by the new you at first. I wasn't always sure that I liked her. But liking is different from loving. During the past few years that we have spent collaborating on this book, I have watched you grow. Perhaps a better word to use would be mature. It has sometimes been difficult for me to accept that you are who you are, that your views are different from mine, and that you are entitled to them. Perhaps it is the mother in me wanting to influence your development in the same way that we influence our own children. I have sometimes felt jealous of your new friends. The ones that you have drawn so close to. Then I have told myself that even if these friends are like sisters to you and even if you can confide in them, I still have something that they haven't got. A blood tie. They could not have gone on the journey that we have been on together, and they could not have achieved what we have achieved or found what we have found. I also ask myself if we would have had this relationship if our lives had been different? We could have turned into the sisters that we see shopping together every week; into the families who turn Christmas and birthdays into obligations. We almost did for a few years. Can you imagine us returning to the cemetery only on anniversaries, birthdays and holidays? As we have matured we have changed. I still feel a responsibility towards you because you are my little sister. But I am happy for you and have come to terms with the fact that being sisters means many different things.

And now we are grown up.

Searching for Ernest has awakened aspects of our past which until now have been dormant. The search has not ended, indeed it may have only just begun. People who read about our journey may begin to remember and rediscover Ernest; those who didn't know him have discovered him; and those who didn't know their own fathers may begin to discover them.

Ending this part of our journey which we have made as sisters means a loss. Over the past decade we have had a purpose which has held us together. We recovered a missing part of our lives. With reluctance we are letting Ernest rest. Now we go on as sisters. We do not have our father but we have each other and we have Lynda.

This is the beginning of our relationship. It is the beginning of how we feel we would like to be, as sisters.

Where do I go when there's no one to turn to?
Feel all alone wondering why I am.
Where do I go when I need familiar?
Woman hold my hand.
Who do I lean on when my legs get shaky?
Eyes cloud over, I can't see my way.
Who lets me know that I'm still walking upright?
Woman hold my hand.
Who laughs with me when I'm feeling silly?
Who skips along, dance the whole night away?
Who smiles with me in my moments of pretty?
Woman hold my hand.
Who binds my wounds when I'm bruised and battered?
By strangers and those daily walking in my life?
Who lets me know I am more than my hurtings?
Woman hold my hand.
Who cries with me when I lose my baby?
By accident, choice or against my will?
Who knows that I am a childless mother?
Woman hold my hand.

Who makes me sing when my voice is silent?
Songs have left me for places unheard.
Who bids me sing when all singing seems useless?
Woman hold my hand.

Mae Frances
Bernice Johnson Reagon
Songtalk Publishing Co.

Select Bibliography

Books

Fryer, Peter, *Staying Power: A History of Black People in Britain*, Pluto Press, London, 1984, reprinted 1988.

Locke, Kath, 'Black People in Manchester', unpublished thesis, Manchester, 1982.

Makonnen, Ras, *Pan Africanism from Within*, OUP, Oxford, 1973.

Marke, Ernest, *In Troubled Waters*, Karia Press, London, 1974, reprinted 1988.

Mendes, John, *Cote-Ce-Cote La: Trinidad and Tobagonian Dictionary*, College Press, Trinidad, 1986.

Sealy, Yvette, 'A Short History of the Trade Union Movement in Trinidad and Tobago', unpublished thesis, Cipriani Labour College, Trinidad, 1989.

Ward, Charles, *No Hardship in Being Black*, Facto Books, 1983.

Newspapers and Periodicals

Birmingham Mercury, Birmingham, 1930–1949.

The Keys, The League of Coloured Peoples, London, 1930–1949.

Manchester Guardian, Manchester, October 1945.

Video

Birmingham, BBC, 1989.

Merle Collins
Rain Darling

'Don't try to get me out, Tisane. This is the only place I sane, because everybody in here supposed to be mad: I like them; is the sane people I fraid. I happy here.'

In these haunting stories by the talented author of *Angel*, Merle Collins returns to her native Grenada to reflect on the ironies, the paradoxes and the tragedies of the lives of 'ordinary' people. These are stories to make the reader weep and sometimes laugh aloud in sheer delight.

Fiction   £4.95
ISBN: 0 7043 4258 8

Angela Davis
An Autobiography

With a new introduction by the author

'I don't know how long we had been sitting in the dimly lit room when Helen broke the silence to say that it was probably not going to get any darker outside. It was time to leave. For the first time since we discovered that the police were after me, I stepped outside.'

With this scene, Angela Davis opens her now classic bestselling autobiography, written when she was 26 years old and already established as one of America's outstanding radical black leaders. Fifteen years on, in a new introduction, she reassesses those turbulent years and her own developing politics.

Autobiography/Women's Studies   £6.95
ISBN: 0 7043 4209 X

Ama Ata Aidoo
Changes
A Love Story

'Ama Ata Aidoo has a remarkable skill for dramatising the
nuances of love and marriage. No one conveys better the
dilemmas of being a modern African woman.'
Margaret Busby

In this lively and touching novel about Esi, freshly separated
from her husband and confronted with the near
impossibility of finding male love and companionship on
anything like acceptable terms, the distinguished Ghanaian
writer Ama Ata Aidoo shows herself once more an
entertaining and unreformed subversive. *Changes* is her
latest novel and will delight new readers and old friends
alike.

Fiction   £6.95
ISBN: 0 7043 4261 8